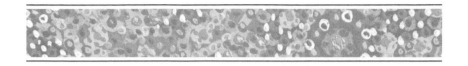

# PRAISE FOR NETTELHORST AND HOW TO WALK TO SCHOOL

## CIVIC LEADERS

"What the Nettelhorst parents have managed to accomplish with so few resources is awe-inspiring. If every school community followed their example, more people would be willing to invest in public education. In our challenging economy, this honest and straightforward blueprint could not be more timely or vital."—Steven Anixter, L&R Foundation

"City parents always have, and always will, make neighborhood schools their highest priority as they work to revitalize their communities. Jacqueline Edelberg has taken this concept to the highest level ever, with magnificent success."—Marilyn Eisenberg, cofounder of the Chicago Children's Museum

"Nettelhorst parents have become experts at forging mutually beneficial relationships with private organizations. This inspiring playbook shows how tenacity, creativity, and infectious enthusiasm can achieve stunning results."—John McDonough, president of the Chicago Blackhawks

"What does it take to turn a struggling neighborhood school around? It shows how a little hope and a lot of community muscle can change a public school overnight. *How to Walk to School* will inspire you to roll up your shirtsleeves, grab a paintbrush, and make your own neighborhood school a place to cherish."—Ron Reason, photographer, gallery owner, journalist, and educator

"So many middle-class families would love to reclaim their neighborhood school, if only they knew how to start. In Chicago, a handful of school communities have followed the Nettelhorst blueprint, added their own unique spirit, and achieved success. *How to Walk to School* should be required reading for stroller moms everywhere."—Terri Versace, parent and founding member of WatersToday

## EDUCATORS

"Chicago's Nettelhorst School is a wonderful example of the implementation of the community school model at its strongest. The Nettelhorst team has crafted a community school that meets the needs of students, families, and community members; engages parents and community members; and maximizes the resources within the building and beyond. The results speak for themselves—student achievement is rising, families are receiving support, and the community is stronger due to the school's presence and participation. Nettelhorst presents a compelling road map for schools hoping to make similar transformations.

All the research and anecdotal evidence shows how community schools have benefited children and adults in communities all over Illinois and across the nation. Students thrive when the parents and community members take ownership for the success of the school. Today's students are tomorrow's wage earners, taxpayers, citizens, and community members. Nettelhorst is proof positive that the community school model can provide a comprehensive and dynamic learning opportunity.

The critical time to act is now—we cannot wait any longer to meet children's needs and improve their chances of success in adulthood."—Suzanne Armato, executive director, the Coalition for Community Schools in Illinois

"*How to Walk to School* has a crucial message for our entire nation during this time of pressing need for education reform, for stepped-up parental involvement, and for high quality, early childhood education. Scholars write reams about school reform and how to do it. However, what they say rarely communicates effectively or reaches those in a position to implement their ideas. Our schools and parents can take vital, understandable lessons from the Nettelhorst blueprint—plus incredible inspiration which is so essential to energizing action. I stand in awe of what this school community has accomplished. "—Laura E. Berk, PhD, distinguished professor of psychology, Illinois State University, and author of *Awakening Children's Minds: How Parents and Teachers Can Make a Difference*

"As principal of Nettelhorst, Susan Kurland made healthy eating and active lifestyles a priority throughout the school. Her work is a shining example of how parents and school leaders can work together to truly create a culture of wellness that educates the whole child. The benefits for children's health, for their learning, and for the entire community are tremendous."—Rochelle Davis, CEO, Healthy Schools Campaign

"If all my schools were like Nettelhorst, I'd have fewer gray hairs. Nettelhorst has hit a home run."—Arne Duncan, former CEO, Chicago Public Schools

"This well-written account is a refreshing break from the polarizing debates over whose responsibility it is to reform public education. Principals can't do it without parents, and vice versa. Nettelhorst's success story is due to a remarkable grass-roots effort that could and should be replicated across the nation; this book offers valuable insight into the process for anyone willing to try."—Diane Foote, MLS, and former executive director, Association for Library Service to Children

"After listening to Susan Kurland and Jacqueline Edelberg tell the story of their collaboration at Nettelhorst, I was impressed. After touring the colorful, beautiful, magical hallways and classrooms of the school, I was blown away. Nettelhorst represents what the research supports: when parents, schools, and communities become collaborative partners, children learn and thrive. Nettelhorst is proof that creative, intelligent stakeholders who come together to care about kids can effect amazing transformations.

In my capacity as an education professor, I supervise student internships at many schools around the Chicago metropolitan area. None of the schools I visit look or feel like Nettelhorst. None of the schools have parents who are so active and are so welcomed by the administration. None of the schools have that same sense of community. In this day and age of school choice and increased adversarial relations, we need to emulate the Nettelhorst model. We need collaboration. We need cooperation. We need community. Nettelhorst has really figured it out."
—Andrea Kayne Kaufman, associate professor, DePaul University, School of Education

## POLICYMAKERS

"Every child in America deserves a stellar education. If you ever wondered what *you* could do to make this a reality, the Nettelhorst road map provides the answers. Ambitious and well written, *How to Walk to School* promises to reframe the debate on school reform. A must read."—John Cullerton, senator from Illinois's 6th District

"Neighbors, parents, teachers, and students have poured themselves into making this little school a place to be proud of. If everyone followed their lead, together we could change the face of public education in America."—Sara Feigenholtz, state representative from Illinois's 12th District

"*How to Walk to School* shows great things can happen when an energetic principal, committed parents, and a supportive community come together to transform a struggling school. It is a must read for anyone interested in how to improve urban education. Kudos to Jacqueline Edeleberg and Susan Kurland for their amazing story."—Tom Tunney, alderman from the 44th Ward, City of Chicago

## PRESS ON NETTELHORST

"A Chicago public school has gone from one of the worst to one of the best ."—CBS 2 Chicago, "Inside a Chicago Public School That's Turned Itself Around," May 4, 2007

"Over the last year . . . local parents have overseen a remarkable transformation at Nettelhorst."—*Chicago Reader*, "A Touch of Class," October 3, 2003

"'If we don't do the kinds of things that we're seeing at Nettelhorst, we will be faced with an entire generation of children who will not be productive adults,' said Dr. Terry Mason, the city's Health Commissioner." —*Chicago Sun Times*, March 21, 2006

"It's a success to make Mayor Daley proud."—*Chicago Sun Times*, "N. Side school fights to attract N. Side kids," April 3, 2005

"The 110-year-old school is in the midst of a renaissance."—*Chicago Sun Times*, "Upgrading Community Expectations," March 4, 2003

"The salad bar at Chicago's Nettelhorst Elementary School . . . is one way the school is promoting healthier choices for students. It also teaches nutrition, has an after-school cooking program, has reinstituted recess, and has dance and physical education classes—the sorts of programs needed at far more schools, children's health advocates say, given the rise in childhood obesity."—*Christian Science Monitor*, "Overweight Kids: Schools Take Action," May 2, 2006

"This 110-year-old public school—largely forsaken by residents of its white, middle-class area north of downtown—is experiencing a rebirth." —*Education Week*, "Community Schools Cooking Up Local Support in Chicago," December 3, 2003

"The Nettelhorst School is a vibrant and dynamic school, but just a few years ago, it was far from being a school of choice . . . in four years, test scores have more than doubled."—PBS, WTTW, "Chicago Matters: Valuing Education, Bake Sales and Beyond," June 6, 2006

"The [Nettelhorst] Parent Co-op is an excellent example of what concerned neighbors can do when they put their heads together and serves as a model other needy schools should emulate."—*Skyline*, "Local Forum," February 20, 2003

# HOW TO WALK TO
# SCHOOL

# HOW TO WALK TO
# SCHOOL

## BLUEPRINT FOR A NEIGHBORHOOD SCHOOL RENAISSANCE

## JACQUELINE EDELBERG
## AND SUSAN KURLAND

ROWMAN & LITTLEFIELD PUBLISHERS, INC.
Lanham • Boulder • New York • Toronto • Plymouth, UK

Rowman & Littlefield Education
Lanham • New York • Toronto • Plymouth, UK

Published in the United States of America
by Rowman & Littlefield Education
A Division of Rowman & Littlefield Publishers, Inc.
A wholly owned subsidiary of The Rowman & Littlefield Publishing Group, Inc.
4501 Forbes Boulevard, Suite 200, Lanham, Maryland 20706
www.rowmaneducation.com

Estover Road
Plymouth PL6 7PY
United Kingdom

British Library Cataloguing in Publication Information Available

**Library of Congress Cataloging-in-Publication Data**

Edelberg, Jacqueline, 1967–
    How to walk to school : blueprint for a neighborhood school renaissance /
Jacqueline Edelberg and Susan Kurland.
        p. cm.
    Includes bibliographical references.
    ISBN 978-1-4422-0000-5 (cloth : alk. paper) —
    ISBN 978-1-4422-0002-9 (electronic)
    1. School improvement programs—Illinois—Chicago—Case studies.
2. School and community—Illinois—Chicago—Case studies. 3. Urban
schools—Illinois—Chicago—Case studies. I. Kurland, Susan, 1945–
II. Title.
LB2822.83.I3E34 2009
371.2'070977311—dc22                                                2009010698

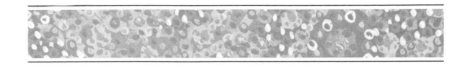

# CONTENTS

THIS BOOK is dedicated to the thousands of volunteers who powered the Nettelhorst revolution; to the community leaders who always fought to put kids first; to the gutsy families who took a leap of faith, and the fine teachers who promised to catch them; and most of all, this book is dedicated to the Nettelhorst students who always, always filled our hearts with joy. We are forever grateful and humbled to be in your company. —Jacqueline, Susan, and Flo

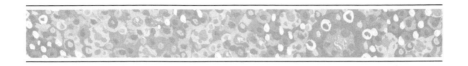

# ACKNOWLEDGMENTS

**M**ANY PEOPLE are responsible for making this book possible, but none more than our dear friend Florence Powdermaker. Flo is one of those moms who took the now-famous Nettelhorst school tour and subsequently joined the revolution. She translated her skills in editing and writing into various communications projects for Nettelhorst, including the school's monthly newsletter and marketing materials. Flo was a natural choice to give our story wings.

No one could have been better suited for the job of crafting this story from scribbles on cocktail napkins to the inspirational account you are about to read. Her talent, wit, and boundless energy lifted our spirits whenever tolerance, caffeine or martinis seemed in short supply. Without her counsel and literary advice, this story might have remained only local legend.

Like everything else in the Nettelhorst reform movement, writing this book has been a labor of love. Flo worked on the manuscript while managing a full time job, a house renovation, and three children under ten. While we all want our children to learn to share, Aaron, Collin, Jamie deserve gold stars. To her husband Andrew: thank you for supporting our project, not just in words, but in deeds.

In addition to being a fine writer and editor, Flo is also a dedicated student of the martial arts. By example, she has taught us the meaning of the tae kwon do principle: *Pil Sung*, "Must Succeed!"

"Never doubt that a small group of thoughtful citizens can change the world. Indeed, it is the only thing that ever has."

— MARGARET MEAD

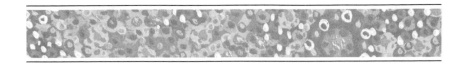

# FOREWORD

MEANINGFUL partnerships between schools and local communities are critical. When organizations and individuals harness their resources to support children and families, both schools and neighborhoods benefit. Students receive the services they need to be successful, parents become more engaged in their children's education, businesses receive the highest return for their investments in human capital, and schools become what they should be—hubs of learning and activity that energize the entire local area.

Community schools do not close their doors after the academic day ends and the last bell rings. Instead, they remain open, providing enrichment and athletic activities, health care, library services, and other resources to children, parents, and the public.

Chicago's community schools—of which Nettelhorst School is the first—have improved at a faster rate than schools in the rest of the district every year since I was appointed superintendent in 2001. These schools have boasted increased civic engagement, improved attendance, fewer discipline issues, and higher student achievement. Through partnerships with corporations, nonprofit groups, and colleges and universities, these schools have been well equipped to respond to the needs of Chicago's most vulnerable students.

In addition to community partnerships, perseverance, talent, and innovation matter tremendously at these—and all—schools. Dedicated parents, skilled teachers, creative administrators, rigorous curricula, and high standards are a huge part of any school's success.

While there are no silver bullets in education, community schools represent a holistic way of confronting the many challenges of improving our public education system. By inviting parents and diverse stakeholders into the school reform effort, we can collectively raise education to the next level in our neighborhoods and across the country.

Providing every community and every child with a great school is not only about education. It's the civil rights issue of our time. Our children have one chance at a quality education. If we do not provide it, we perpetuate poverty and social failure; but if we do provide it, we open the doors of opportunity and prosperity to every child who walks through them.

—Arne Duncan, former superintendent, Chicago Public Schools

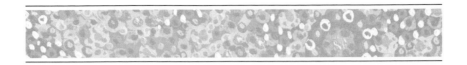

# INTRODUCTION

THIS IS the story of an entrepreneurial principal and visionary neighborhood parents who took a leap of faith together and transformed an underutilized, struggling urban elementary school into a successful, vibrant institution. It outlines how Susan Kurland, Nettelhorst's new principal, and Jacqueline Edelberg, a neighborhood artist and mom, brought together a school community to create a stimulating and lasting relationship.

The Nettelhorst story takes place in a middle-class Chicago neighborhood, but it is about improving all schools for every child. It demonstrates how creativity, hard work, perseverance, and passion can make an astounding difference in a building and in a community. The Nettelhorst story showcases the powerful effect of simply asking parents, local businesses, and community members to get involved. In the heated debate over school reform, the Nettelhorst blueprint compels politicians and policymakers to reexamine the viability of the neighborhood school model. The Nettelhorst vision can be realized in any community—obviously, the players will be different, their abilities and expertise unique to their situation, but their level of engagement can be equivalent because of their common desire to put their children first, regardless of race, class, or socioeconomic status.

This book speaks to middle-class, urban parents, frustrated by a public school system that, due to many factors, cannot provide excellent education to *all* children. In spite of so many top-down, visionary, educational initiatives, few children actually experience their benefits. The new state-of-the-art magnet school becomes meaningless to the luckless kid who lives just down the street but loses the required lottery or fails the entrance exam, and thus cannot gain admission. In other words, when a neighborhood school converts to a selective enrollment school, oftentimes local middle-class families who so desperately want to be admitted find that they can't enroll their children, and parents are then forced to seek other options. Theoretically, the increased competition for talented students should spur neighborhood schools to step up their game, but sadly, most principals don't rise to the challenge.

Consequently, one unfortunate byproduct of parental choice is the inevitable resource drain that ensues every time an innovative magnet school opens its doors. When middle-class parents choose to send their children to magnet schools outside of their neighborhood, whatever resources they might have directed toward their own local school get siphoned off to another locale. One might think that all this crisscrossing energy balances out across the school attendance areas, and that the system enjoys some kind of happy equilibrium of parental engagement, but this is not the case.

Parents typically are not able to support a magnet school as much as they could support their local neighborhood school. Just as parents whose children are bused from overcrowded schools face barriers to participation, parents whose children attend magnet schools far from home find impediments to their involvement. Challenged by geography, these parents cannot volunteer regularly or make social connections with other parents as easily as they could if the school were located close to home. Long commutes tend to limit chance brainstorming sessions or spur-of-the-moment volunteer projects. Imagine how much more engaged these same talented and energetic parents could be if they simply walked their children to and from school everyday.

A successful neighborhood school would likely see more community support than an equally successful magnet school with a bused-in population. Owners of local businesses that benefit from a strong family customer base (e.g., grocery and retail stores, restaurants, ice cream parlors) are more likely to donate goods or services to a public school if they sense their investment will translate into increased exposure or revenue. Neighborhood groups are more willing to invest in capital improvements or special events if they believe that the neighborhood will benefit from their efforts. As everyone's property value increases exponentially when every child in the district—not just the brightest or the most fortunate—has guaranteed admission to a high-quality public school, neighbors become more likely to donate to the school or support local programs.

America has been told that "it takes a village to educate a child." The essence of a village is the near proximity in which people live, work, and raise their children. It would be remarkable if city dwellers took responsibility for educating every child, but such unbounded altruism is unrealistic. Most urban villagers are egocentric actors who need to see the personal value in their investment. Neighbors can see the positive effects of a successful neighborhood school almost immediately.

The Nettelhorst renaissance proves that the neighborhood school model remains viable. Until the middle class abandoned the city for the suburbs in the early sixties, the neighborhood model succeeded for over a century. This model continues to work in suburban areas, not necessarily because suburban schools have superior teachers, broader curricula, or even more money (although that certainly helps), but largely because bounded entry forces the school to be responsive to its constituents. While Chicago's Board of Education prides itself on school choice, for most prospective parents, selective magnet schools prove to be elusive or untenable. Parents may apply to any selective magnet school of their choice; however it is up to the luck of the draw or the caliber of the competition which of those schools will offer their child a golden ticket. Because the demand for selective magnet schools so far outstrips supply, parents rarely get their first, second, or third choice, or find that siblings have been admitted to different schools, sometimes clear across town. A great many savvy parents would *choose* public education if it would only *choose* them.

Discriminating families can hardly be faulted for rejecting an inferior product; many signs suggest that neighborhood schools are not the best choice. Why can't these schools compete with their more prestigious magnet and charter school cousins? By law, all public schools in Chicago should be on the same footing. Every school is expected to reach the same educational standards and cover the same basic curriculum, and must answer to both the Board of Education and the teachers union (except for charters that don't need to hire union teachers or follow most board structures). Chicago Public Schools (CPS) gives all schools comparable financial support (except for charters that receive even less money per student). The most telling difference seems to be that neighborhood schools must accept every child in their immediate attendance boundary, regardless of aptitude. Could non-selective enrollment be the Achilles' heel of the neighborhood school model?

Nettelhorst's bounded entry was, in fact, pivotal to the school's dramatic turnaround. In just five years, Nettelhorst transformed itself from a school the neighborhood loathed, ridiculed, or ignored into a vibrant community hub that propels families to move—in droves—*into* the school's guaranteed attendance boundaries.[1] Prospective parents living outside the geographic borders, in an effort to improve their chances in the random computerized lottery for the rare open seat, now send letters to the principal infused with high praise about their tour of the school or descriptions of how their family's charitable work or other qualifications make their children ideal candidates for admission. The once scorned "Nettelhorst District" became desirable real estate, virtually overnight.[2]

Now, picture this alternative outcome. Imagine if these same middle-class families, rather than relocating to another school district or taking chances with flattering overtures to the principal, redirected their resources, energy, and creativity into reinvigorating their own neighborhood school. How many schools can be reinvented and how many children can, as a result, gain a high-quality education? This book offers a blueprint for how parents, communities, and public schools can create successful partnerships and the effective, nurturing, educational environment that all children deserve. The Nettelhorst model reveals how a visionary principal and a group of dedicated parents worked together to achieve astonishing results for an entire community.

This story speaks to parents, educators, policymakers, business owners, and neighbors who have become impatient with the sluggish progress of America's school reform. The Nettelhorst movement bucks the conventional wisdom that schools must first solicit "buy-in" from *every* stakeholder before taking action. Reform can be messy and unpredictable. Yet, if cities are serious about attracting and retaining middle-class families, schools must move faster and take calculated risks to make public education viable. The fact of the matter is that it is going to take more than bake sales to pull schools out of their current predicament. Quite simply, principals need to dramatically re-envision how public schools conduct business, and middle-class parents must be willing to roll up their sleeves and get to work.

Chicago's East Lakeview families were prepared for the challenge and willing to work for the school they deserved, but they had scarcely an idea as to how to begin. Thanks to the efforts of eight gutsy women and one open-minded principal, Nettelhorst developed a plan to deliver a viable school that would become one of Chicago's best, in record time. The road to transformation was both maddeningly difficult and shockingly easy. Their story of revitalization can be adopted by almost any neighborhood across the country.

This blueprint documents the nuts and bolts of how parents and educators can establish a relationship based on honesty, commitment, trust, and joy. It details how stakeholders in the school community can develop chemistry, solidify relationships, and overcome personal and institutional challenges. In a climate of scarce funding for public education, it explains how schools can identify external resources and how parents and students can become financial advocates. Wherever a school finds itself on its journey to success, the Nettelhorst blueprint can help by inspiring the neighborhood to reclaim the great public school it deserves.

# ONE

# DREAM A FUTURE

## IDENTIFY OPPORTUNITIES

PICTURE TWO real-life examples set in gentrifying neighborhoods in Chicago. In the first scenario, local parents convene a town hall meeting with the principal of their underutilized public elementary school. The families demand answers. The principal adamantly explains that despite the poor test scores, her school is still an appropriate choice. A representative from the public school board supports her argument with statistics and what the parents perceive as bureaucratic double-talk.

The frustrated community members, hearing no viable solutions to the school's declining educational performance, become angry and cite their high taxes and diminished property values. Some question why their local alderman is MIA. One mother cradling an infant yells, "Just fix the damn place!" Another man complains that the principal is incompetent and should be fired immediately. The meeting further dissolves into name-calling, ad hominems, and bad blood. Everyone walks away wondering why no one in the room has taken responsibility for finding solutions.

In the second scenario, a group of parents hold a private meeting with the principal of their underutilized local public school. The well-meaning parents discuss the fact that although the school's test scores have improved over the past several years, few neighborhood families are enrolling their children at the school. In case the principal does not fully appreciate just how poorly the community regards his school, the group confides that even the local alderman has given up hope that the school will pull out of its nosedive.

The neighborhood parents offer to volunteer their time and skills to help the principal transform this institution into a school of choice. As successful doctors, attorneys, government employees, and business consultants, these parents have considerable expertise to share. Despite their heartfelt appeal, the principal, unwilling to take a risk with his school, thanks the parents for their candor and generosity, and suggests other, "more suitable" schools for their children. The meeting ends. The parents, stunned and demoralized, leave with the realization that they now face the daunting process of private school interviews and magnet public school applications. The local public school drifts ever further into disrepair.

Versions of these two scenarios play out frequently in cities across the United States. Yet parents' and principals' inability to work together for the betterment of neighborhood schools makes little sense, given the steep challenges that face American education. State and federal funding for education continues to decrease. No Child Left Behind legislation threatens to close underperforming schools. Stretched budgets leave schools understaffed with underpaid, disheartened teachers, overcrowded classrooms, and crumbling infrastructures. The end result is that far too many students across the country are not receiving the education they need and deserve. But all too often, the very principals who desperately need help rebuff well-intentioned parents who pledge themselves to addressing these challenges.

Surely principals are aware that family engagement is one of the critical factors—if not *the* critical factor—in determining their school's success or failure. Principals must know better than anyone that they need all the help they can get—which begs the question, why are struggling principals so reluctant to embrace local parents who offer to volunteer their time, energy, and expertise?

It is easy to imagine why the principal in the first scenario would choose not to work with the hotheaded parents. After all, a principal's job is so taxing that she would be foolish to wittingly add more trouble to her already full plate. But why would the principal in the second situation refuse the help of solicitous parents who want to create a collaborative environment that would benefit everyone?

Part of the explanation lies in a principal's need for self-preservation. Most parents last set foot in an elementary school the day they graduated, and few understand a principal's responsibilities, daily routine, or work environment. Hollywood movies such as *Dangerous Minds* and *Lean on Me* don't help matters. Successful teachers are rarely mavericks like biker jacket-clad Michelle Pfeiffer, who connects with her students by teaching them karate moves and Bob Dylan lyrics. In the off-screen world, most teachers are mild-mannered, hard-working individuals who love children and try their best to teach a state-approved curriculum, day after day. The most successful ones have learned, by hard experience, to shut out a cacophony of background noise.

Furthermore, most principals rarely arrive on the scene as renegade outsiders, creating order by busting heads. In the real world, the teacher-turned-principal rarely roams the halls like Morgan Freeman, baseball bat in hand. Rather, most principals barricade themselves in their private office from early morning until late at night, soldiering on in the face of increasing responsibilities and ever-shrinking resources.

Often public school principals work in an environment that feels like a full-tilt pinball game, juggling teachers, staff, students, parents, maintenance needs, and the school board. They attempt to strike a balance and provide direction from their perch in the main office, an environment that all too often resembles a stock exchange pit, an air traffic control tower, or a twelve-step meeting, all within the span of a single morning!

To complicate matters, almost everyone who walks through the door genuinely believes he or she is the "center of the universe," deserving of the principal's immediate and unwavering attention. Imagine the ingredients that comprise the typical public elementary school cocktail: five hundred self-centered children, one thousand emotional parents, one hundred underpaid and overworked teachers and staff, plus scores of prospective parents, bureaucrats, community members, and policymakers, *each and every one a self-appointed expert on education.* Even superior principals find it difficult to prioritize the competing needs of all these egos, especially given the school's decentralized power structure. Even when the school office seems preternaturally quiet, the climate remains adrenaline-fueled and potentially volatile.

The new principal must navigate this super-pressurized environment, at least initially, moving around both marked and unmarked landmines. The inherited staff is unique and complex, prone to dysfunction and opposed to reform. To make matters more challenging, the principal is constrained by a dizzying array of local, state, and federal laws and a school board's often arbitrary and capricious will. Given all the unavoidable demands with which principals must contend on a daily basis, they are understandably reluctant to take on any additional liabilities. Principals have become wary of involved parents because "offers to help" will almost certainly hijack their valuable time and energy. Occasionally, such a "kind offer" may serve as window dressing to a simultaneous appeal to the district's superintendent or legal department. Consequently, many principals, even fairly successful ones, have constructed impenetrable boxes around themselves. Who could blame them for employing such defense mechanisms to stay afloat?

## ACKNOWLEDGE THAT THE SCHOOL CAN'T GO IT ALONE

In Chicago's East Lakeview community, the neighborhood elementary school cycled through periods of decline and renewal right along with the neighborhood writ large. From the 1920s through the 1950s, Nettelhorst was among the most prestigious elementary schools in Chicago, but fell into severe decline during the suburban flight of the 1960s. When East Lakeview struggled to bounce back in the early seventies, a group of gutsy neighborhood moms, led by Marilyn Eisenberg and Marianne Schenker, sparked a grassroots reform movement to reinvigorate Nettelhorst.

The feisty moms recruited in neighborhood parks, hosted prospective parent coffees in Marilyn's swank Lake Shore Drive apartment, raided school-age children from nearby preschools, shooed the prostitutes and pushers off the school grounds, and packed Nettelhorst with neighborhood students. While the movement successfully repopulated the school with middle-class families, reform was fleeting; three consecutive teacher strikes and an administration change heralded a mass exodus that left the school floundering for more than twenty years.[1]

By the late 1990s, the East Lakeview neighborhood had bounced back in force, but its neighborhood school never recovered. Nettelhorst was shunned by not only the neighborhood's middle-class families, but by *all families*. In 1999, 242 of East Lakeview's children were enrolled in a CPS elementary school; however, not a single one went to Nettelhorst. *Not one.* Many of these neighborhood children even gathered on Nettelhorst's front playlot in the early morning, waiting for a yellow bus that would whisk them away to a public magnet school elsewhere in the city.

How did Nettelhorst fall into such a terrible state? In 1995, the Chicago Board of Education instituted a new policy that designated Nettelhorst as "underutilized" because so few families in East Lakeview were choosing to enroll their children in the school. At the time, many argued that the board should close all underutilized schools, or at least the schools situated on the most valuable real estate, and sell the property to developers. Instead, the board decided to change the neighborhood schoolhouse model. Rather than shutter underutilized neighborhood schools, the board elected to bus students from overcrowded schools in typically unsafe neighborhoods to otherwise empty schoolhouses in relatively safe neighborhoods. It then filled any remaining seats with special education students culled from throughout Chicago.

For Nettelhorst, this new board policy translated into a death sentence. Every day, a total of fourteen buses delivering 630 regular and special education students from seven different school locations descended on the school. Strategically, schools do not opt to bus out their better-performing—and usually better-behaved—students; the group transported to Nettelhorst offered no exception to the rule. The bused-in student population, of which 90 percent came from families with incomes that fell below the poverty line, were displaced from their neighborhood to a distant school that they had little interest in attending.

Although Nettelhorst tried to provide a quality education to the bused-in student population, circumstances made success almost impossible. Because the CPS school bus schedules were rigid, most of Nettelhorst's students could not take advantage of any of the after-school programs the board had offered in an effort to boost academic achievement. Even if the after-school programs had a chance of working, most students' home environments were not conducive to academic success; parents were, for the most part, absent and unreachable.

Compounding matters, each year the students' legitimate "home school" would recall its students and send a new batch of kids to Nettelhorst's door. In 1998, the year before Susan Kurland took charge of Nettelhorst, the school suffered a 49 percent mobility rate. In real terms, this meant that Nettelhorst inherited a difficult and different student population each year. The resultant lack of stability created a recipe for underachievement; test scores revealed only 30 percent of Nettelhorst students were performing at or above grade level.

The challenge of the high student mobility rate was further exacerbated by Nettelhorst's revolving door of administrators. In the 1990s, Nettelhorst chewed through *seven* interim principals. Chaos reigned at the school. The Nettelhorst teaching staff may have been "headless," but its fists punched and its legs kicked. Left without effective leadership, some teachers tried to create some semblance of order but often worked in opposition to one another's efforts. Meanwhile, others flagrantly disregarded all instruction, rules, and timetables. Combined, the teachers presented an almost insurmountable challenge to anyone who attempted to bring cohesive leadership to the school.

This stalemate between administrators and staff effectively ostracized the local community, who had little idea if anyone was really in charge of the school at all. Local politicians had essentially given up any hope that the school would be able to rebound. Nettelhorst was failing its leaders, teachers, parents, community, and most tragically, its students.

And yet, Nettelhorst's Local School Council (LSC), the small group of elected teachers, parents, and community members charged with oversight of the school, believed in Nettelhorst's potential. The LSC worked diligently to improve Nettelhorst by spending the school's discretionary funds on an all-day kindergarten when most CPS schools only offered half-day programs. The council hired teachers to decrease the teacher/student ratio and purchased bilingual materials to meet the needs of Latino students. Despite these efforts, the lack of any viable leadership left the school without a strategic plan for how to get the school on the right track. Recognizing this fact, the board removed Nettelhorst's acting principal in 1998, and assigned not one, but two administrators "to get the school under control."

In 1999, the LSC hired a new principal to lead Nettelhorst, but he rescinded his acceptance just a few months before the start of the school year. In hopes of finding the right hire, the LSC turned to the Leadership Academy and Urban Network for Chicago (LAUNCH), a professional development program designed to groom leaders for Chicago's schools, to recommend some potential candidates. Despite the fact that LAUNCH was a brand-new program that graduated brand-new principals, the LSC believed that the program's intense training and ongoing professional development would more than compensate for a candidate's inexperience. LAUNCH recommended Susan, who came with a great deal of public school experience: She taught early childhood education in New York and Chicago and led a new CPS high school as associate principal. When the LSC offered her the job at the eleventh hour, in spite of Nettelhorst's rocky history, Susan accepted the opportunity to create the school of her dreams.

Over two years, Susan worked hard to change the neighborhood's negative perception of the school. The boarding/disembarking scene at Nettelhorst merited special attention. Energetic children quarantined on a bus for over an hour rarely emerge on their best behavior. Whenever Nettelhorst's fourteen school buses arrived on the scene, the school population emerged in a wave of violence and profanity. In an effort to build community support, she instructed teachers to bring students into the building as soon as the buses pulled up to the curb. At the end of the school day, she accompanied students back onto their assigned bus. When her presence on the school grounds failed to "quiet the troops," she appointed student bus monitors, instituted assigned seating, and personally began to ride the buses.

Having made strides with the students' conduct outside the school building, the school could focus on improving behavior displayed within Nettelhorst's walls. To help eliminate distractions, the school instituted a uniform policy (white tops and navy bottoms). To help students see fair and consistent consequences, Susan uniformly enforced the CPS Discipline Code and removed unruly students from classrooms when they displayed inappropriate behaviors. After a few months of consistent discipline, the students learned their limits. Nettelhorst's halls quieted down and students became more engaged in their schoolwork.

Despite the demands of a standards-based curriculum, Susan believed that unstructured playtime was essential to healthy and happy development. At a time when most public schools had eliminated recess entirely, Susan convinced teachers to sacrifice a planning period in order to offer recess for every student, every day. Even in cold temperatures, everyone bundled up and went outside to play. In seriously inclement weather, she instructed teachers to walk students through the entire building for ten minutes before landing in the lunchroom. Exercise and unstructured social play created healthier, happier children and more receptive learners.

When the behavioral issues began to stabilize, Nettelhorst could then more easily mainstream its special education students. While the special education children certainly benefitted from large, individual classrooms (as opposed to cramped rooms in crowded schools), they were effectively isolated from mainstream, regular education children due to the student population imbalance. Nettelhorst had a two-to-one ratio of special education to regular education classrooms. This separatist mentality not only negatively affected the students, but also discouraged collaboration among the teachers. Susan vowed to remedy Nettelhorst's approach by creating opportunities more conducive to inclusion, academic progress, and new teaching partnerships.

As Nettelhorst's student population stabilized, Susan ensured that special needs children visited regular education classrooms whenever possible, sometimes becoming permanent members of the class, as mandated by the Individualized Education Program (IEP). In some cases, special education students would spend part of the day studying certain subjects in one classroom, and then migrate to another classroom to receive more individualized instruction in other subjects, when necessary; it soon became completely natural for children to come and go. The regular education students not only helped the special needs children, but they also became more insightful, patient, and compassionate.[2]

Once she brought discipline under control and improved the school's approach to special education, Susan could focus her attention on raising the academic bar. In her first year, the LSC successfully lobbied to become an International Scholars Magnet Cluster School—a neighborhood school with a special focus, such as world language, fine arts, reading, or science—that the board would grant extra teachers endorsed in special subjects. Because the program mandated integrated units, teachers now had a compelling reason to collaborate in grade-level teams. As teaching became more supervised, some of the teachers elected to leave, allowing Susan to recruit individuals who believed in the new vision for Nettelhorst.

## ASSERTIVE LEADERSHIP

Before Susan's inherited teachers would be willing to collaborate, Nettelhorst needed to become a place of trust, encouragement, and reflection. Although the school's teaching climate was dysfunctional, by and large, the actual teaching was not wholly unsatisfactory. Teachers, though dispassionate, showed up to work every day and made a reasonable effort to educate their students. Susan assumed that the school's low scores and high mobility rates were symptomatic of the school's inconsistent leadership rather than a toxic teaching climate. It didn't take her long to figure out that Nettelhorst suffered from both concerns.

In hopes of building a functional team, Susan began by opening her door wide—really wide—inviting teachers into the planning process to edge them out of their complacency. Following conventional wisdom that suggests new principals shouldn't make too many dramatic changes during their first year on the job, Susan kept most of Nettelhorst's established protocols and room assignments in place. However, if the LSC expected her to jump-start Nettelhorst's sluggish academics, her teachers needed to start collaborating. Given Nettelhorst's tumultuous history with administrators, teachers formed cliques and adopted a laissez-faire doctrine as they waited for each incumbent principal's tenure to end. The teachers assumed that Susan's regime would crash and burn, just like all those that came before, and they behaved accordingly. Their attitude had to change or Nettelhorst could never improve.

Susan hoped that increased socialization would help teachers feel more comfortable with her and with one another, so she expanded her new open-door policy even more. She welcomed any opportunity to "break bread" with her team. Any holiday was an excuse for a celebration. For Halloween, Susan donned a costume and held a teachers' breakfast at the school. At Thanksgiving, she invited everyone to a feast at a neighborhood restaurant, where they shared stories of thankfulness with one another. To observe the winter holidays, she reserved a party room in her apartment building and invited the team for a soiree. Susan tried to make her staff feel special at the holidays; she gave each a personal note with a little gift, such as a coffee mug and gift certificate for the winter break, flowers at Valentine's Day, or a chocolate bunny for Easter. While not everyone was won over by these small gestures of gratitude, many teachers appreciated the thought.

Despite the increased socialization, her teachers still had a long road to travel before their relationships would mature into collaboration and mutual respect. Nettelhorst's teachers, like most individuals, were reluctant to embrace change. Schools of education train teachers to focus on their own students, and the isolating public school environment only reinforces this myopia. Collaboration and cooperation might be possible, but out of habit, most teachers hoard materials and shut their classroom doors. When teachers do emerge from their classrooms, most find comfort within their established cliques circumscribed by class, age, or ethnicity.

During her first year, Susan carved out an extra preparation period from the schedule so that teachers would have the time to greet one another, plan, and discuss any concerns. Unfortunately, these meetings became a painful exercise. When Susan was present at the meeting, teachers quickly turned it into a gripe session, openly airing personal resentments. In a few instances, some teachers became so bitter with one another that they could barely manage to be in the same room and demonstrate civility. When Susan couldn't attend a meeting, the teachers discussed few matters of consequence, if they bothered to assemble at all.

In her second year, Susan recalibrated the school's preparation periods in hopes of fostering greater collaboration and professionalism. She formalized sessions by changing the venue to the assistant principal's office and asked her new assistant principal to supervise them, taking attendance, recording minutes, and so forth. On paper, it seemed like a good approach—without the principal's presence, the grade-level teams would be less prone to vent or posture, and would be more likely to collaborate on grade-level integrated units. But without the principal's explicit direction, the new assistant principal allowed these participants to engage in inappropriate behaviors at the meeting. As news of their shenanigans traveled throughout the school's rumor mill, the staff became even more alienated and divisive. By the end of the year, it became apparent that Nettelhorst could manage without that assistant principal altogether.

While working to bring her teaching staff on board, Susan also attempted to engage parents in their children's academic goals. Sending home letters had little effect, so she encouraged creative home/school partnerships through a range of activities, including special reading challenges and monthly family nights. In spite of her efforts, Susan experienced only mild success in engaging a disjointed and transient school population.

The LSC recognized that if Nettelhorst was going to improve significantly, it needed to attract and maintain a stable population from its immediate attendance boundary. While the school's long-standing, state-sponsored free preschool program for "at-risk" children (now called Preschool For All) ran almost to capacity with neighborhood children, and an all-day kindergarten might have seemed like an attractive incentive, few chose to remain for kindergarten. In 1999, Susan and the LSC tried a different tactic, lobbying CPS to become one of the first thirteen schools to open a tuition-based preschool (TBP). As part of Mayor Richard M. Daley's initiative to make universal preschool services available to all children and their families, CPS created a citywide tuition-based preschool program (TBP) which placed heavily subsidized, fee-based, all day, state-of-the-art preschool classrooms in neighborhood elementary schools. In addition to helping kids gain the skills to hit the ground running in kindergarten, Mayor Daley hoped that the program might also help lure the middle-class back into the public school system. Susan and the LSC hoped that neighborhood families would whet their appetites with the TBP and be so awed that they would elect to stay on for elementary school.

Contrary to expectations, few neighborhood children enrolled in the TBP, and even fewer remained for kindergarten. Susan was mystified as to why neighborhood families continued to shun Nettelhorst despite steadily rising test scores. Clearly, Chicago's neighborhood children were attending public schools in increasing numbers, but neighborhood families were still not opting to register their children at Nettelhorst. If Nettelhorst was truly on the upswing, why didn't the neighborhood see its value?

## THE ROSCOE PARK PARENTS

The Lakeview families who frequented Roscoe Park, a small city play-lot located just a few blocks from Nettelhorst, also faced school angst, but from a parental perspective. Jacqueline Edelberg, who had left a university teaching position to raise her daughter, had logged hundreds of hours sitting around the park's sandbox with other young parents. It was here in this outdoor sanctuary, where parents often developed close friendships that Jacqueline learned most families were wrestling with the same educational questions she was trying to answer.

Initially, Jacqueline consciously chose to ignore all the desperate park chatter about schools. Parents angling to get their kids into prestigious private schools seemed to miss the point of education, and even childhood, for that matter. She rejected the idea that her children needed a celebrated kindergarten noted on their curriculum vitae to be considered for an Ivy League university one day. But as Jacqueline really began to listen to the park conversations, it became clear that most of these anxious parents were not social climbers seeking the perfect school for their progeny; rather, they were rational people who, quite simply, found themselves with few academic options. The Roscoe Park parents all faced the same conundrum: Finding an elementary school that met their standards *and* would admit their children was a much more challenging proposition than they had imagined.

Some of the park parents assumed they would need to leave the city to ensure their children received a quality education. The suburban school districts overall seemed to have better test scores and more funding allocated to primary school education. But most of the parents were reluctant to leave the homes and social networks that they had established in Chicago. They had discovered that raising babies and toddlers in the city was not the nightmare their parents or suburban friends had predicted; in fact, it was a lot of fun. If parents could navigate the harsh winter with stroller and sanity intact, Chicago offered an astounding array of activities for young children and parents alike. Why shouldn't families have the same opportunities if they chose to remain in the city after their child turned five?

For those families intent on remaining in the city, their next decision centered on the type of school—public or private. Most of the park parents were products of public schools themselves and were generally supportive of public education. But both options were given due credence.

As well-informed individuals, the parents could mount credible, philosophical arguments both for and against each type. They voiced endless lists of factors important to them in selecting a school, whether public or private, including safety, location and transportation, cost, diversity, parental involvement, academic rigor, class size, and so on. Aside from concern for their child's well-being, parents also worried (albeit in whispers) about how their personal social standing, networking opportunities, and peer group would be impacted at one school versus another.

As the park parents bounced back and forth between the merits of public and private schools, they noted that both seemed to offer some distinct advantages that might just as easily turn into liabilities. On the one hand, public schools might be sound training for real world situations, but the real world could be awfully scary; perhaps private school would better protect impressionable children. On the other hand, the "homogenous bubble" of private school could become a real problem if the air inside turned sour. While private schools typically have smaller class sizes than public schools, a class of fifteen students or fewer could become problematic if one's child suddenly didn't fit in. Private schools are not required by law to accommodate students with special needs, so it would be unlikely that a learning or behaviorally challenged student would dominate a classroom; however, if one's child were to develop a disability midstream, a private school might kick him or her out, regardless of how much money the parents had invested in the institution. Private schools didn't have to bother with state testing, so teachers would not be wasting time "teaching for the test," but the lack of accountability could mean that students were advancing in grade level without mastering key skills. As parents could hardly predict what kind of kid their five-year-old would become, they were hard-pressed to say that private school was categorically better than public or vice versa.

The public versus private school debate became even more fraught with anxiety as parents weighed their financial and familial situations— potentially needing to leave or return to a full- or part-time career, having additional children, caring for elderly parents, managing a health crisis, coping with a divorce, or blending a family. As Chicago's elite private schools can cost upwards of $20,000 annually per child, most families needed to carefully weigh the costs and benefits of a private school education.

Even the park parents earning six-figure salaries wondered if the actual education private schools offered was really worth the high tuition; although a quality education was priceless, how difficult could it really be to teach a kid to read or subtract? To the untrained eye, much of the typical kindergarten day seemed to involve eating lunch, playing outside, going to the bathroom, and gluing dried pasta on construction paper. At the risk of looking cheap or selfish, many park parents questioned whether paying private school tuition should take precedence over taking the family out to eat or on vacation, to say nothing of saving money for college or retirement. And, of course, why shouldn't parents be the beneficiaries of their own astronomical property taxes?

Even if the cost of an elite private school wasn't a concern, admission could be problematic. Siblings of current students or children of alumni or big donors were first in line for enrollment. Every year, wistful parents found themselves competing against thousands of other families (all seemingly wealthier and better-connected) for a precious few kindergarten spots. In a front-page article in the *Chicago Tribune*, a mother echoed the all-too-familiar lament: "I've spent more time on this process [of finding a school for my five-year-old twins] than I did trying to get into college or law school. There is so much stress and uncertainty right now, I feel sort of panicked about what is going to happen."[3]

After exhaustively comparing the costs, benefits, and shortcomings of a private education, most Roscoe Park parents ultimately voiced their preference for public schools for their kids. But finding a public school that offered a safe environment and quality education *and* granted admission was a tall order. The park parents began to research their public school options. Because CPS guarantees admission for students living within a particular school's geographic zone, many families consider relocating to another area of town to gain entrance to the public school of their choice. Rather than resorting to such drastic (and costly) measures, families could opt for the application and testing process associated with magnet schools or, if feasible, leave their fate to a principal's discretion to permit their out-of-area child to attend.

Parents who hoped to clarify the public school options with research found volumes of convoluted and contradictory data. Even the park's savviest policy wonks had difficulty understanding Chicago's various public school offerings, ranging from neighborhood, magnet cluster, traditional magnet, classical, Montessori, gifted, and specialized charter. The data available on the CPS and State of Illinois websites proved overwhelming as parents attempted to decipher student test scores; dropout, mobility, and truancy rates; socioeconomic demographics; and teacher retention statistics, salaries, and qualifications. Certainly, the best- and worst-performing schools were easy to identify. But the vast middle ground—where most public schools seemed to fall—was daunting to chart.

And then there were the rumors. The Roscoe Park parents had heard them all. That some schools would accept families that could talk or buy their way in; that some families applied to literally dozens of public schools, yet didn't get in anywhere; and that some parents resorted to fraud by misrepresenting their home addresses to place themselves within one of the city's "golden school districts," thereby guaranteeing admission or at least improving their odds.

City officials seemed somewhat delighted by the heightened public school frenzy. Upon hearing that some parents lied on their magnet school applications, Mayor Daley remarked that "it may be the first time in the history of Chicago" that savvy parents are aggressively angling to get their kids into Chicago's public schools. "Usually they are fleeing, going to private schools, going to the suburban areas."[4] After decades of urban flight, the very idea that Chicago was experiencing a reverse salmon run on inner-city public schools was cause for celebration.

Of course, frustrated parents were hardly toasting the system's good fortune. In spite of the rush on select magnet schools, parents wrestled with the "Emperor's New Clothes" rumors: that safety issues or threats of gang violence were kept quiet; that test scores had been doctored; that results weren't actually indicative of student performance because the tests were culturally biased. Some parents pointed out that a passing Illinois Standard Achievement Test (ISAT) test score only indicated that a student had passed *minimum* standards. If a significant percentage of a school's population was failing to meet even minimum standards, certainly there were more issues than met the eye. Many argued that a magnet school's high scores were less an indicator of stellar teaching and more an inevitable consequence of a self-selecting applicant pool.

Other parents could overlook a public school's mediocre test scores, choosing instead to believe that parental involvement was ultimately the most significant indicator of a student's impending success or failure. But again, how would one measure parental involvement? How much parents volunteered in their child's classroom? How many books they shelved in the library? Or was it just being supportive and nurturing at home? After all the questions, arguments, and counterpoints, most Roscoe Park parents believed that parental involvement at home, in all its many guises, was the single most important factor in determining their child's success or failure.

Yet while the park parents vowed to support their children, how could they be sure that all the other students' parents would provide the same nurturing environment in their respective households? Surely a teacher could prop up a few unsupported students, but what if the numbers were more like a third, or half, or even more? What if *all* the other classroom parents didn't read to their children, didn't limit television watching or video game playing, or fed them an endless diet of sugar and junk food? Was parental involvement contingent on income, language, culture, or neighborhood? The parents had hunches and prejudices, but hardly anything definitive or impartial.

The Roscoe Park parents determined that, in light of all these concerns, their best chance of success would be to enroll their children in one of the city's reputable magnet school programs. Surely this would be the best option for a family that wasn't fortunate enough to own the right piece of real estate to take advantage of guaranteed admission inside a choice school's boundaries. Regrettably, that must be the same thought most Chicagoans have because, as the park parents learned, it wasn't unheard of for a parent to submit applications to roughly twenty public magnet schools across the city to secure a spot for her child.

Because the competition for spots at choice magnet schools is so intense, parents would accept an offer from any school that accepted them. Whatever the magnet school's particular focus—foreign language, fine arts, applied science, Montessori, classical, or gifted—is largely irrelevant given that all the choice magnet schools have great teachers, solid test scores, and involved parents. And parents were willing to do whatever it took to have their child attend one of these select institutions, including driving round-trip clear across town or putting her child on a multiple-hour bus ride. Most park parents believed Chicago's magnet schools presented the best and only public school option.

## MAGNET SCHOOL ATTRACTION

CPS admits students to these choice public schools by lottery or testing (with some weight for proximity), and needless to say, the competition for spots is fierce. For example, admission to LaSalle Language Academy, a magnet school with a long-established reputation, receives roughly one thousand applications for approximately sixty kindergarten spots each year. At Drummond Montessori, a new magnet school in Chicago's Bucktown neighborhood, 995 children applied for just thirty-six spots, which translates to a mere 4 percent acceptance rate.[5] Comparatively, it is more likely that a high school senior will gain admission to Harvard than a kindergartener will find a place at one of Chicago's top public magnet schools.[6]

The Board of Education justifiably prides itself on the high quality of its magnet schools, but it did not originally intend for these schools to cull the cream of the crop from the city's applicant pool. The board created Chicago's first magnet school in the late sixties as a way to avoid forced desegregation by the federal government. The school would select a student population by computerized lottery that would mirror Chicago's racial and socioeconomic demographics. The magnet school stopped acting as a "social equalizer" in the early eighties, when the then-governor's daughter attended the city's inaugural magnet school. Almost overnight, notoriety (and increased funding) helped catapult the new magnet school to become *the* choice public school in the city.

In response to the heightened demand, the board created several more magnet schools, but changed the criteria for admission from racial quotas to test scores or random computerized lottery (with some proximity advantage, as well). As these new magnet schools began to flourish, it became just as competitive to secure a kindergarten spot in them as it did in the original magnet schools. A handful of schools might each accept fewer than fifty students. In short, Chicago's entire five-year-old population was in competition for a few hundred choice kindergarten spots, many of which were already gobbled up by sibling preferences or inscrutable, discretionary principal selections.

As these original magnet schools became more and more popular, two problems emerged. First, these schools were siphoning off the best and the brightest from the citywide elementary school-age population as neighborhood schools languished. And second, the cost of busing hundreds of students from all over the city became prohibitive. Because magnet schools were created in the sixties precisely to avoid the costs and disruptions of citywide busing, both the board and the mayor were keen to see busing come to an end.

The cash-strapped board sought to remedy this situation in the late nineties by creating special magnet cluster schools. The board would choose five neighborhood schools in close proximity to each other, give them a special focus (such as foreign language, fine arts, reading, or applied sciences), and group them into a cluster. These neighborhood magnet schools would draw from their immediate attendance boundary, just as regular neighborhood schools did, but as Chicagoans seemed to be clamoring for choice, parents also had the option to apply to another school in their magnet cluster. Each neighborhood magnet school could choose to accept up to 15 percent of its students through a random lottery, although parents would need to provide their own transportation to get their child to and from school. The board hoped that parents would remain in their own neighborhood and choose the school that most appealed to them—the language school for their budding linguist, the fine arts school for their promising artist, and so forth. If CPS infused neighborhood schools with more resources and a special focus, it gambled that these new magnet cluster schools would share the same appeal as traditional magnet schools.

Unfortunately, the board invested little energy in promoting these new-and-improved neighborhood schools, and the public did not perceive them as magically transformed. Guaranteed admission to a retooled neighborhood school hardly offered enough incentive if parents believed the school's overall education was substandard. Unlike a magnet school that the board initiated from scratch, neighbors already knew their neighborhood school, and a simple change of letterhead or a new marquee could not easily win their trust or respect.

Few parents were interested in having their children specialize in kindergarten and could hardly be expected to switch schools in third or fourth grade. If their child seemed gifted, most discriminating parents would likely choose one of Chicago's selective test-in magnet schools (crossing fingers and toes that one of the schools would choose them back) over the nonselective magnet cluster school down the street, despite its "special" focus. The presence of a couple of endorsed teachers in one subject area was hardly enough to level the playing field.

If parents hoped to get their eighth-grader into a private high school or an established magnet high school, a strong, well-rounded elementary education would be a prerequisite. Consequently, families who were determined to remain in the city *and* send their children to public school resolved to take their chances and play the traditional magnet school lottery game.

While some parents simply relied on the luck of the draw, others worked hard to guarantee admission at one of the established magnet elementary schools. While magnet cluster schools didn't mandate diversity, the computerized lotteries seemed to favor minority applicants; hence, some children "suddenly developed" intriguing racial ancestries. Some magnet schools were rumored to accept families who could sweet-talk their way in. Everyone in the park had heard the story of Jack Grubman, the notorious Citigroup stock analyst who traded professional favors to get his preschool-age twins into a prestigious New York City private school. The park parents wondered how Grubman would finagle a spot at one of Chicago's choice public schools.

What extra effort would it really take to get a kid into one of Chicago's competitive magnet schools? Beyond writing the principal a stellar "loved the tour" letter or donating money, it was unclear exactly how much parents needed to do. Should parents join the local school council? Shelve books in the library? Tutor kids after school? Sew costumes for the school play? It seemed absurd for parents to invest significant time or money in a public school that their children didn't even attend, even more so when the school was located many miles from their home. The prospect of angling for admission to one school was bad enough, but to compound it by ten or even twenty schools was enough to make any sleep-deprived parent of a toddler apoplectic.

Even families of means seemed to have trouble successfully navigating the magnet school application process. Rumors circulated among the Roscoe Park parents. One savvy, well-connected family applied to over thirty public schools but met with nothing but rejection. Another family bought a new million-dollar home spitting distance from a choice magnet school, and despite spending hundreds of dollars at the school's fundraiser, was rejected for kindergarten. When choice public schools turned away parents who could sing arias for their supper, what did that say about everyone else's chances?

To make matters worse, park parents found that the magnet school admissions notification schedule was maddeningly out of sync with the private school timeline. Glitches with the computerized lottery left each magnet school mailing acceptance letters on different dates. Families were left contemplating whether or not to risk declining a private school spot for a magnet school admission that might never materialize. Still other magnet schools would offer spots on the waiting list just weeks before school started in September, the time when private schools were finalizing nametags on cubbies. One notorious urban legend cited a particular magnet school's protocol to telephone accepted applicants over a two-day period; like waiting for the cable guy, anxious parents would stay home because if they missed their appointed telephone call, their child's lucky spot would be given to the next one in line. While Chicago's selective magnet schools were excellent public school options, few parents had the means or stomach to understand, much less play, the system and gamble that their child might not get in anywhere.

Given the cost of private school, the uncertainty of admissions, the problems associated with public school (including budget cuts, high class sizes, low test scores, busing, concerns of violence, closures, and strikes), No Child Left Behind, and a state ranked forty-ninth in primary education state funding per student, it is no wonder why so many Chicago families decide to move to the suburbs before their kids reach kindergarten.

## NETTELHORST, EAST LAKEVIEW'S NEIGHBORHOOD SCHOOL

For the families who chose to live in East Lakeview, their neighborhood school, Nettelhorst, was not viewed as a viable option. It may have been a neighborhood magnet cluster school, but that did not matter to the East Lakeview residents who—if they had any familiarity at all with the school—had only encountered rumors of drugs, low test scores, and gang violence. And, for years, the fighting and profanity that surrounded Nettelhorst's students as they exited or boarded the busses did nothing to alleviate that image. Even though almost all of Nettelhorst's students were whisked away on buses in the afternoon, the perceived threat of shoplifting was so great that some stores posted signs prohibiting unaccompanied students from entering. "The Nettelhorst Problem" was a regular talking point on meeting agendas for neighborhood and community associations. At that time, if someone had asked a neighborhood parent, "Would you consider Nettelhorst?" the possible responses ranged from blank stares to outright laughter.

Jacqueline didn't know a single park parent who had ever ventured inside Nettlelhorst, but just looking at the building and its grounds seemed to confirm the rumors. Physically and structurally, it looked like a school ought to look: On the front of the red-brick, three-story building, a delicately carved Art Nouveau stone placard read "The Nettelhorst School, Erected by the Board of Education: 1892." However, that is where the pleasantries ended. Ample sheet-metal signage on the playground warned trespassers against dogs, loitering, and ball playing. All the exterior doors were dingy, brown, and locked. Come evening, aluminum florescent light fixtures from the fifties gave the schoolyard a sterile penitentiary feel.

During the school day, most of the school's ugly, beige, vinyl window shades were drawn. On the rare occasions when they were open, the three rooms at street level told a series of sad tales. In one room, random assortments of furniture pressed up haphazardly against the windows. Another classroom revealed a handful of teenagers hanging around without any apparent adult supervision. And the third window on the first floor—the only porthole through which one could witness students learning—revealed a well-supplied but claustrophobic preschool in which classes seemed to be held only sporadically.

As long as anyone could remember, at the exact instant the final school bell rang—a loud buzzer that could be heard half a block away—the building exploded like a firecracker. Hoards of unruly youths spilled out onto the sidewalk to board the fourteen yellow buses that choked the local streets with exhaust fumes. All the while, pedestrians quickly and instinctively crossed to the other side of the street.

In the summer of 2001, Jacqueline's husband had promised to undertake the necessary research to find a school for their two-year-old daughter but became too busy at work, and the job fell into Jacqueline's reluctant hands. Private school was an option, but now that Jacqueline was expecting their second child, double tuition payments would have been a stretch. Even if they could swing the finances, private school admission wasn't going to be a cakewalk. It only took fifteen minutes researching CPS on the Internet to realize that applying to public school was just as daunting. In a curious mixture of optimism, desperation, and laziness, Jacqueline decided to visit Nettelhorst to see if the neighborhood school was indeed as awful as she had heard.

Pushing her daughter's stroller around the school grounds, Jacqueline stumbled upon an open, unmarked side entrance. The heavy, gray metal door swung open to reveal an old man behind an even older school desk. The security guard stopped reading his paper long enough to wave her inside. But a moment later, a large woman bounded around a corner and screamed at her to leave *immediately*. Jacqueline left in bewilderment. Perhaps one needed an appointment to visit the school? If so, scheduling one would be problematic. No one ever seemed to answer the phone. Intrigued by the mystery, she made it a point to call every day at various times for a week, at which point some kind soul finally answered, and Jacqueline made an appointment to meet the principal the very next morning.

Jacqueline invited her Roscoe Park friend and neighbor Nicole Wagner, who had a eighteen-month-old daughter, to accompany her on the visit. On the preceding evening, the two women sat in the hot summer air and wondered what had happened to the little school since 1893 to bring it to its current state. Had there been a mass exodus? Did the board make a mess of things? Was the principal a witch? A large crane was situated on the school property; had the old building finally been sold to make way for condominiums? Maybe it wasn't even a proper school at all. The only way to find out for sure would be to go and check it out. The next morning, Nicole and Jacqueline left their daughters in the care of a babysitter and walked to Nettelhorst so that they could meet with the principal and, if nothing else, definitively rule out their closest public school option, which, they felt certain, was probably no option at all.

Dr. Kurland—Susan, as she introduced herself—jovially walked the two young mothers around Nettelhorst. The first thing Jacqueline and Nicole learned was that the school was not in danger of being closed; rather, the giant cranes were present to replace the school's 120-year-old roof that had recently collapsed. The good news was that the cave-in had happened on a Saturday, so no one was injured. The bad news was that the school had been shuttered for six months while CPS made repairs. In spite of the construction debris, they scampered around the battered building, carefully ducking under the yellow caution tape to look at various classrooms and the soon-to-be-completed gymnasium (a happy by-product of the roof incident). In her makeshift office, the principal proudly shared a large three-ring portfolio, each page highlighting a new program she had implemented for Nettelhorst's students. Clearly, Susan loved the building and was very proud of her students.

After her three-hour show-and-tell session, the principal bluntly asked the women, "What do I have to do to get your kids to come here?" Quite stunned, they looked at each other for a moment before replying, "We'll come back tomorrow and let you know." What Jacqueline and Nicole didn't realize at the time was that most principals would not have entertained advice from energized neighborhood parents interested in making "improvements," let alone come right out and asked for it. Susan understood that Nettelhorst suffered from the classic chicken-and-egg dilemma: The school needed to improve to attract neighborhood families, yet it needed that same community to help direct, enable, and sustain that change. Like any principal, she was pulled in multiple directions and her time was at a premium. She tried to engage her teachers as much as possible, but she knew that the school still needed more. Instead of being hurt, angry, or threatened that the neighborhood parents didn't appreciate how far the school had already traveled, she took a risk of faith and asked them to dream big.

## CREATE A WISH LIST

What would have to be in place in order to convince the neighborhood to return to Nettelhorst en masse? To answer that question, Jacqueline and Nicole returned home, parked their daughters in front of *Dora the Explorer*, and began to brainstorm. They tried to imagine what the ideal elementary school might look like, how it would feel, and what programs it might offer. Although Jacqueline had taught at the college level and Nicole had already researched several Chicago schools, neither had any direct experience in elementary education beyond their own experience as children. So they started by perusing Nicole's carefully organized stack of glossy promotional brochures from the city's top private schools. Together, the two cobbled together an elaborate wish list: low teacher/

student ratios, accelerated academic programming, foreign language instruction, conceptual math, unfettered parental access, beautiful classrooms and public spaces, and stellar enrichment programs. If Nettelhorst wanted to be a choice, a *real* choice, it would need to offer the neighborhood a comparable product.

They assembled a long list of what they planned to present the next day. But could the school deliver, or would this be a futile pipe dream? The principal had made progress with the school, that was certain, but the results, as illustrated by her "brag book," would not be sufficient on their own to compete with Chicago's best schools. Yet the school held promise. The old building had great bones. The principal was straightforward and ingratiating. Although there were no students or teachers in the school, given summer recess and the roof calamity, Jacqueline and Nicole could easily imagine happy sounds filling the halls. All in all, it was not a terrible picture.

Allowing themselves hope, they put the last of the items together for their Big List:

## Big List's Headings

- Stellar academics
- Low teacher/student ratio
- Recess, physical education, sports
- Healthy, organic lunches
- Music, art, drama
- Foreign language
- Involved, passionate, dynamic teachers
- A safe, clean, and beautiful environment
- Parental involvement
- Extracurricular activities
- On-site, before- and after-school care
- Fun playground, landscaping
- Well-stocked, cozy library
- State-of-the-art technology

- A well-equipped science lab
- Fun traditions, like a spelling bee or a spirit week
- An open-minded administration and great leadership
- All-day kindergarten
- Nice kids

The first two headings on the list were deal breakers. Without rigorous academics and a low teacher/student ratio, Jacqueline and Nicole figured Nettelhorst would be a lost cause.

The next day, the young mothers returned to the school, as promised, to deliver their heartfelt manifesto. Susan read through their extensive wish list, thought for a moment, and simply said, "Well girls, let's get moving, it's going to be a very busy year."[8]

In a crush of excitement, Jacqueline and Nicole found themselves obsessed with the prospect of "fixing Nettelhorst." They earnestly began the process of identifying the school's issues and discerning potential solutions. From their initial impression, they felt that the school suffered from both physical and perceptual problems. The physical issues—such as a dreary interior and an empty library—seemed relatively easy to fix. If the walls were gray, then a fresh coat of colorful paint would go a long, long way. Surely there were companies that donated books, computers, and other needed resources. However, assuming for a moment that park parents could overcome these significant challenges, Jacqueline and Nicole suspected that changing the community's deeply entrenched negative perception would be a tall order to fill.

## ASSESSMENT

Jacqueline and Nicole wondered if they really had the energy to deal with cleaning up something that took so many years to decline. Surely the process of changing a school's ingrained culture is difficult; maybe it would be easier to simply begin with a clean slate? Perhaps a charter school would be easier to get right from the start since it could sidestep the union and cherry-pick a team of highly dedicated and motivated teachers. However, the process of launching a charter school relied on political approval and could take years to get off the ground; the park parents only had a matter of months before their children reached kindergarten age.

Another possibility would be to start a new private school. Some park families were in the process of starting a small private, parochial school, and listening to their war stories was harrowing. Assuming for a moment that the park parents could start a private school from scratch—a huge assumption—families would still face the challenge of being able to afford the tuition of the very school they founded. Except for the advantage of guaranteed admission, founding a private school didn't seem to solve anything. Nettelhorst, despite its many flaws, already had an enormous infrastructure, a staff of teachers and administrators, essential supplies, and at least a bare-bones operating budget. It became the logical choice to attempt to fix Nettelhorst, whatever its problems might be, rather than to try to open a brand-new school.

Clearly, changing the community's deeply entrenched negative perception of Nettelhorst would be an uphill battle: *everything* from public relations to marketing would need to be tackled concurrently. While the East Lakeview neighborhood had a grittiness and diversity that tended to attract open-minded families, they knew that parents wouldn't be willing to risk their children's education. Most of the families in Roscoe Park had infants and toddlers; Nettelhorst needed to become a viable option within a very short time span if it hoped to capture these children who were rapidly approaching kindergarten. If it failed to improve significantly, families would take their chances with the other options: magnet school lotteries, private school applications, or, finally, suburban alternatives. In addition to whatever real problems needed to be addressed within the school, Nettelhorst's serious image problem was going to be a real kicker.

## MAKE A GAME PLAN

Because no blueprint existed for how neighborhood parents might turn a neighborhood school around, Jacqueline and Nicole created their own action plan. How did other public schools become successful? How did they manage to recruit parents? How many neighborhood students would a school need to enroll for it to reach a tipping point? How could parents lead a reform movement at a school when their children didn't even attend it? How could the Nettelhorst reformers know their efforts would not be in vain? Where would they even start in such a daunting process?

After touring a nearby successful elementary school, Jacqueline confessed to its veteran principal that she and other parents were thinking of fixing their own neighborhood school, Nettelhorst. She assured Jacqueline that Nettelhorst's principal knew exactly what was wrong with her school and wanted it to be better even more than they did. Nettelhorst wasn't fundamentally any different than her "good" school: Both were roughly the same size, both were situated in vibrant neighborhoods, and both were "CPS magnet cluster schools," meaning, neighborhood schools with a special focus and the ability to admit students from outside their attendance boundary if not filled to capacity.

The principal then whispered a singular pearl of wisdom: Her school had something that Nettelhorst didn't have—parents. "Get parents in, and you can achieve anything. Sit down with your principal and make a game plan together. Aim for the moon. If you don't reach it, you're sure to land pretty close anyway."

While the nearby school took years to turn around, flipping Nettelhorst could be done in a matter of months if Jacqueline could recruit eight women to work *together* with Nettelhorst's principal. If the women put their minds to it, their neighborhood school could become the kind of place they all desired. The principal waxed poetically about a little place in Italy where all the townspeople banded together to support a local school, spawning an educational philosophy called Reggio-Emilia. What if everyone in the Lakeview neighborhood showed up to teach their craft: the bakers, cobblers, Thai noodle makers, and so on? Nettelhorst could be amazing.

The Roscoe Park parents didn't necessarily need a utopian City on a Hill; they simply needed a normal public school, no grander than their own childhood elementary school. If the Roscoe Park moms failed to fix Nettelhorst in their limited time frame, surely they would be no worse off than if they did nothing but sit in the park and fret. What did they really have to lose?

Starting the process, eight neighborhood friends agreed to captain or cochair teams that most closely mirrored their education and work experience: infrastructure, curriculum, enrichment, special events, public relations, and marketing. They proclaimed themselves the Nettelhorst Parents' Co-op and adopted the motto: "We do more during naptime than most people do all day." Every two weeks, the team captains, who nicknamed themselves the Roscoe Park Eight, promised to reconvene at the Melrose, a popular diner across the street from Nettelhorst.

As the team captains formulated an attack, they quickly calculated that Nettelhorst had only nine months to become a viable option for their children. Working backward in the calendar from June (the month they resolved to tackle Nettelhorst), they identified the key dates involved in their ridiculously short time span. Mid-May: All parents with children turning five must commit to kindergarten for the following year. Mid-March: Private, parochial, and magnet schools notify families of admission decisions. Mid-December: Applications are due for private, parochial, and magnet schools. October through December: Families shop for schools in earnest. Backing into the timeline this way, the team captains realized that if Nettelhorst had any hope of filling a kindergarten class the following year, the Roscoe Park Eight had just seven months to get the school ready to be seen by neighborhood parents for the first time. Consequently, the community needed to get to work on Nettelhorst a full year *before* any neighborhood children might arrive.

While a mid-January open house was already late for most shoppers, come March, countless families would be rejected from the private and magnet schools and forced to contend with the inevitable "What are we going to do now?" conversation. In their moment of desperation, Nettelhorst would have to be viable, or at least compelling enough that they would make alternate, temporary arrangements for their children, biding their time until the school would be good enough. If most park parents moved on to other schools for their children, the initial energy to reform Nettelhorst would likely dissipate. The team captains seemed to have a very narrow window of opportunity.

Even with all the time in the world, several park parents warned that the Nettelhorst revitalization campaign was doomed to fail. They suggested that the public school system was so dysfunctional at every level that no amount of good work would outweigh the problems of a hostile administration, some less-than-able teachers, and overcrowded, underfunded classrooms. A low point came when a young mother, who had spent five years teaching in a CPS high school, happened into the park with her toddler. Although it obviously pained her to say it to a group of clearly enthusiastic parents, she asserted that neighborhood parents could not just march in to fix a public school and expect that everything was going to turn out peachy.

The mother contended that Nettelhorst's principal had sold them on a pipe dream. Public schools receive money each year based on the number of students in attendance. Nettelhorst's principal was only interested in filling seats to augment her annual budget. Far better that park parents hear it from her now as opposed to two or three years down the road, when their kids would be in second or third grade, with little to no chance of getting into a private or selective magnet school.

Katja Dierks, one of the regular park moms rallied to their defense. "I'm originally from Germany. And there you would fail. No one would ever think that parents could go in and change a public institution. But here in America, you have the idea, and boom, you run with it. It is an amazing energy, *ja*? Why not?" The park parents could think of a lot of reasons "why not," but Katja was right. What was the harm in trying? Who was the audience they would disappoint? Discriminating toddlers? The park parents were likely already getting flak for their choice to raise kids in a shoebox or leave a career to stay home, so what difference would one more foolish choice make in the scheme of things? If the project proved untenable, surely they would know it within months, not years, and could chalk up their efforts to philanthropy and move on.

Behind the scenes, it was clear that the local politicians had their own doubts that the revitalization campaign could succeed. When Jacqueline first approached the now-former alderman with the Co-op's plan to revitalize Nettelhorst, he suggested that she would be better off just sending her children to the nonselective neighborhood public school in his ward that already was successful. When she told him the story of how she had visited *that* school and that its principal had encouraged her "to gather eight women, and build a dream with Nettelhorst's principal." the veteran alderman actually laughed out loud. He replied that he had been trying to fix Nettelhorst for years, but, truth be told, the little school was beyond hope. However, if the park moms wanted to give it a go, he promised to support their efforts any way he could. At this stage, Jacqueline wasn't sure what the alderman could do to help, but thanked him for his time and vowed to take him up on his kind offer after the Roscoe Park Eight figured out a game plan.

Back at the park, the team captains filled their teams with the names of as many friends (and friends of friends) who showed even the slightest interest in helping to renovate Nettelhorst, and in a matter of weeks, they managed to recruit over two hundred parents to join their fledgling movement. The captains simply changed their standard opening salvo to the parent at the next swing from, "Gee, your daughter's tights are adorable," to, "Hey, there's a group of neighborhood moms trying to fix Nettelhorst. Want to help?" More often than not, the accosted parent would say that she had little time and no idea what she could possibly offer, but sure, she would help in whatever way she could. They would continue to push swings back and forth, and back and forth, and talk about the fate of public schooling, a conversation that might continue for hours.

Inevitably, another dedicated volunteer joined the ranks. If the team captains hoped to showcase the school to neighborhood parents in just a few months, they were going to need help, and a lot of it. So they gathered names and telephone numbers and e-mail addresses on little slips of crumpled paper, recruiting for their little revolution with all the gusto of an underdog political campaign. The most difficult part of organizing park parents was that mommies had crayons, sidewalk chalk, and wipes, but no one ever had a pen.

# TWO

# CHEMISTRY

## Capitalize on Desire

IF NETTELHORST hoped to attract neighborhood parents, it
needed to conjure up some chemistry—and fast. Whereas parents
might be willing to overlook the unappealing facility of an established school, Nettelhorst had no such reputation upon which to bank.
The school needed to be more than just clean and well-run; it needed
to radiate creativity, quality, and warmth. Nettelhorst had great bones:
soaring twenty-foot ceilings, large double-hung windows, and dark
wooden moldings. Because of the roof calamity, the century-old school
smelled of paint and construction dust, but also of chalk, modeling clay,
and pencils—the kind of aromas that would immediately transport one
back to the schoolhouse days of long ago. As beautiful as the school
once was, Susan needed to take a good hard look at the building
through the eyes of a prospective parent who lived in the East Lakeview neighborhood—someone who was likely well-educated, discerning, badge-conscious, and highly skeptical of Chicago's public schools.[1]

### SPRUCE UP THE EXTERIOR

Some of the most important improvements to Nettelhorst's exterior were
relatively simple and inexpensive. The school needed to raise the vinyl

window shades so that the neighbors would see a school "in action." The teachers whose classrooms faced the street needed to leave their lights on at night. Such action would not be wasting electricity; a lit building would only result in a marginally higher electric bill, and it would help to market the school and increase security. To make the school more inviting, the school needed to remove most of the negative outdoor signage that warned against loitering, trespassing, ball playing, and the like. It was laudable that Susan had already replaced the boarded up door surrounds with glass in order to better display school flyers, but if neighbors did not take the time to read the neon orange posters, they might reasonably assume the city had finally condemned the building. Simply changing the paper color would radically change the perception. When neighbors passed the school, even if they didn't have children, they needed to see a part of the community that was bright, happy, and welcoming.

The exterior doors also needed immediate attention. Unlike Jacqueline, most prospective parents would not have the persistence to walk around the school for fifteen minutes trying to figure out how to gain entrance. Fortunately, the school was already on the same page; a teacher had just received a grant to create a Nettelhorst School mosaic that would be installed above the front door. The Co-op had all the exterior doors painted blue to match the incoming mosaic and flanked the main entrance with two spiral topiaries.[2] A local lighting store added warmth and style by donating wrought-iron lamps for every door to replace the cold 1950s aluminum florescent lighting. Simple improvements made a marked difference: For the first time in over twenty years, Nettelhorst officially looked open for business. If prospective parents wanted to enter the building, at least there was no longer any signage that told them to get lost. And although the security camera barely worked and no one might be in the office to buzz parents in, at least now they could locate the school's front door.

## GUSSY UP WITH A ZERO BUDGET

When Nettelhorst's roof collapsed, the school needed to empty the library, and Susan seized the opportunity to renovate it. Friends of Nettelhorst (FON), the school's long-established fundraising arm, offered a king's ransom of six thousand dollars to buy new carpeting. Because it was their first major infrastructure project, the Roscoe Park Eight asked if they could try to renovate the library themselves—with a budget of *zero*. Susan thought this was a fine idea, and told them to proceed with their plans and keep her posted. They would only have six weeks to get the library ready in time for the first day of school.

The curriculum team insisted that fixing the library was the school's most pressing challenge. Although Susan concurred that all activity and learning should center in the library, it was hard to believe her given the facts on the ground: Nettelhorst's library had functioned without adequate resources or even a proper librarian for years, and the dysfunctional LSC had managed to suspend student borrowing privileges entirely. The infrastructure team inherited a cavernous seventy-by-thirty-foot space, completely devoid of furniture, computer equipment, books, and saddled with potentially hostile oversight. Surely there wouldn't be a better litmus test for the principal's educational vision or openness to work with outsiders. If Susan failed to deliver on the library project, the Roscoe Park Eight unanimously agreed to chalk up their efforts to philanthropy and move on.

If a school's library was so critical, why was Susan willing to risk such an important space as the Co-op's first major project? For starters, there wasn't really that much at stake: The library was empty and essentially nonfunctional. If the Co-op failed, the FON had already allocated funds for new carpeting, and Susan would be no worse off than when she started. Plus, the experiment would have six weeks to incubate more or less unchallenged. She figured that the library project offered an excellent opportunity for the neighborhood parents to demonstrate their vision, work ethic, and follow-through skills.

So, how could the co-op parents make good on their promise? The answer was surprisingly simple: The infrastructure team simply cracked open the local phonebook and began to cold-call merchants. A typical phone call to a store manager went something like this:

"Hi! I'm with the Nettelhorst Parents' Co-op—you know . . . Nettelhorst . . . it's that little public elementary school on the corner of

Broadway and Melrose. Have you heard of it? No? There are two hundred families in the neighborhood who are trying to fix the school, and, well, you see, the school's roof collapsed—didn't you notice all those giant cranes all summer? Yes? No, no, the building wasn't sold to developers. We are trying to get some angel to donate some [paint, carpeting, labor, padding, chairs, rugs]. You can? Great! When can we come and pick it up?"

Some merchants said no emphatically, explaining that times were tough, or that they paid too much in property taxes already, or that they needed to go through corporate channels. However, many said yes, if only to get the mom to stop begging and attend to the poor, neglected child audibly fussing in the background. Understandably, merchants couldn't give a substantial amount of any product, but most could give a little, perhaps something that might be languishing on their shelves anyway, if the school promised to come and get it.

In exchange for the merchant's donation, the parents offered to distribute promotional material within the school community and to include the merchant's contact information in a Nettelhorst resource book that would be distributed to all the parents in the school. The school was also willing to send a letter to the merchant for tax purposes. With so much going on, the Co-op and the school predictably fumbled on sending thank you notes, and the promised resource book never materialized. Thankfully, however, donors only half-expected that their gifts would result in anything tangible beyond good karma (in later years, the school would be able to do more to recognize its donors via mentions in newsletters, the website, the school directory, etc.).

After only one month of begging and foraging, the Co-op witnessed an inspired library renovation. The 2,100-square-foot space, once bare and sterile, became charming and whimsical, awash in azure blues and white, billowy, painted clouds. Co-op parents had tremendous latitude to realize their aesthetic vision. The team also kept up its end of the bargain by keeping the principal abreast of the progress and seeking her counsel. The team found that Susan was remarkably open to unconventional ideas. A claw-footed bathtub could become a private reading tub? Sure! A sailboat with an orange sail docked in the center of the library? Land, ho! Susan was game for anything that seemed child-friendly, teacher-supportive, and aesthetically pleasing.

As soon as the parents began to renovate the library, it became clear that the school's veteran engineer held almost as much power as the principal. Nothing could happen to the school's infrastructure without both of their approval. With the library project, and every subsequent effort, reformers found the engineer to be remarkable; on his own time, he supervised volunteer workers, even on the weekends, at night, and after school. He also picked up and organized donations to the school and helped co-op parents navigate the strict codes of the Chicago Fire Department and the unwritten codes of Nettelhorst's teaching staff. The veteran engineer loved Nettelhorst, perhaps more than anyone, and encouraged volunteers to respect the building's integrity. Most importantly, he made working on the building a pleasure for anyone who wanted to lend a hand.

When the last of the painters finished working, reformers scrambled over Labor Day weekend to set up all the new furnishings and restock the bookshelves in time for school to start. Because of the roof accident, CPS granted funding so that teachers could set up their classrooms a full week before school began; however, only a handful of teachers chose to return early. Without teachers to help them, co-op parents intuitively organized and restocked the new library, as if dressing props for a movie set, and hoped and prayed that some informed person might show up later to reorganize the space into a functional room. Thanks to so many community volunteers, at least it looked like a library.

In hindsight, the absence of teachers before the official start of school actually worked to the parents' benefit. For the first few weeks, the Co-op did not have teachers looking over their shoulders, critiquing or fighting their every move. Some of the über-critical teachers might very well have argued that the library design scheme was untenable because blue was not conducive for reading, billowing clouds were distracting, or sailboats and cast-iron tubs posed safety hazards to students.

With only Susan and the engineer to please, the co-op parents could create a library, bounded only by their imagination and what materials they could beg, barter, or salvage. After six weeks of effort, scores of volunteers had created a beautiful space that would be ready for a librarian, if indeed the school ever hired one. In any case, Nettelhorst's library was finished in time for school to start.

With the success of the library renovation under its belt, the infrastructure team systematically began to tackle the enormous school methodically, classroom by classroom, hallway by hallway. When the Roscoe Park parents arrived during the summer, Nettelhorst's walls were bare, but by October, after the students had come back to school, the hallways were covered with laminated clip art, cereal advertisements, and pithy motivational posters. Susan turned a blind eye when the co-op infrastructure team brazenly removed all printed images that might repel its target audience.

The school needed to reassure prospective parents, especially the sophisticated park mavens, that their children would only encounter routine, garden-variety problems in public school. Arguably, the school's state-issued posters that admonished children to "Say no to drugs!" or "Stay in School!" were not inherently offensive; middle-class kids are no more immune to the dangers of drug addiction, gangs, smoking, truancy, hepatitis-C, or lice than any other child. However, the Co-op believed interested parents would likely assume that the school was rife with miscreants or would bristle at the implication that their precious child would require a poster to stay out of juvenile court. While there wasn't anything wrong with the state's poster that encouraged students to "Read!" skittish parents might assume that little reading was actually occurring.

With the promise that the Co-op would repaint all the hallways in short order, Susan reluctantly agreed to remove any displays that did not showcase student work. Prospective parents were grasping at straws as to how to evaluate a school for their child, and they would take cues from what they were familiar with—student displays of learning. Like everything else, first impressions were all important. For example, if teachers didn't present student work on their hallway bulletin board in a sophisticated way, neighborhood parents would assume that students were stupid or poorly taught or both. The Co-op insisted that the hours teachers devoted to decorating bulletin boards with scalloped borders, die-cut letters, and pithy motivational phrases was not only a colossal waste of time, but counterproductive.

Teachers would be better served to display their student's work directly on the walls with tape. To make itself comparable to the successful private schools in the area, Nettelhorst should show prospective parents happy, authentic, child-made artwork on the walls accompanied by a teacher's well-written explanation of the project. This new approach would feed the park parents' seemingly boundless appetite for documenting their growing children. Nettelhorst could score bonus points if teachers displayed photographs of children at work or adorable, child-dictated sentences, such as, "This is a tiger swallowing an airplane!"—Samantha, age five, or, "I want to be class president because I know how to tie my shoes!"—David, age six. While these visual clues might not be enough to convince parents that Nettelhorst offered a sound education, they would at least buy the school some additional time to make its case.

As the infrastructure team targeted each renovation project, it asked many logistical questions. When parents entered the school, where would they store strollers or hang their coats? When waiting in the office, where would they sit? How would parents entertain their toddlers while at the school? Where would they change a diaper? The team also considered the students' needs in their planning. Even the tiniest nook could become a comfortable and innovative place for learning, so long as the engineer was satisfied that the decorations would pass the fire department's strict safety codes. In every room, designers tried to create spaces that would encourage community building and facilitate the home-school connection.

The infrastructure team could readily transform even the smallest space into a joyful environment because Susan was open to new ideas and willing to embrace change. In a study of contrasts, at a nearby school parent reformers had orchestrated an elaborate neighborhood volunteer paint day, soliciting a staggering amount of donated materials. However, when the school's principal arrived at Home Depot to approve their chosen paint colors, he torpedoed the entire design scheme in front of the store's manager, leaving everyone at a loss for how to proceed.

The principal was so belligerent and closed-minded that the neighborhood reformers not only abandoned their painting project, they abandoned their reform movement altogether. Of course, the principal's last-minute rejection of their selections was not really about paint color. Why, they wondered, should they devote hundreds of hours to improving a school if its principal was not appreciative and willing to go along for the ride? If he could not imagine a lavender hallway, what did that say about his ability to envision the kind of school they wanted to build for their children?

While Nettelhorst's principal and engineer were on board for change, predictably, not everyone was overjoyed by the transformation. In some instances, frustrated staff members even sabotaged projects. Contrary to the accepted wisdom that effective change requires consensus and buy-in, the infrastructure team, under the leadership of the principal and engineer, was able to formulate an action plan and make their shared vision a reality. The parents suspected that everyone would come to like their new surroundings eventually, but given their accelerated time schedule, there was little time to hold hands or take votes.

While parents tried to bite their tongues, their bulldozing approach remained in force even as the school evolved. For example, fast-forward five years: When the board offered matching funds to buy new playground equipment, Susan only consulted the gym teacher, the counselor, the landscape architect, the playground designer, and the core co-op parents. Even within this limited group of key players, it was a struggle to find common ground. Some didn't want to part with precious open space, regardless of how spectacular the new equipment might be. Others suspected that older kids find all play equipment boring. Some feared that teachers wouldn't be able to supervise recess effectively. Some wanted more time so that the whole school could weigh in on the decision. All these competing opinions held value; however, if the school hesitated or didn't present a united front, the board would rescind the offer. In the end, Susan opened the discussions to the larger school community; however, she weighted her decision based upon expert advice and the knowledge that aesthetic choices are always highly personal and often controversial.

In all projects, the infrastructure team tried to capitalize on Nettelhorst's most salient feature as an International Scholars Magnet Site—the celebration of world cultures. The global theme influenced every space. Before long, Nettelhorst had its own French bistro, English living room, Moroccan salon, African camp, Latin American town square, Indian market, American pop art gallery, and Polynesian beach.[3] At times, the team feared that the school might turn into an amateurish theme park, but somehow the renewed spaces seemed neither silly nor contrived.

After the artists finished their work, public spaces continued to evolve and inspire. Without bulletin boards, teachers easily layered students' artwork on top of murals. The relationship between murals and student work is symbiotic. For example, after kindergartens read Marcus Pfister's *The Rainbow Fish*, the teachers displayed their colored foil and construction paper school in the Atlantis hallway; dioramas of the Serengeti lined the African hallway; solar system dioramas lined the space school hallway, and so forth. Homey touches and knickknacks spontaneously appeared in the kitchen and in the various seating areas. The hallways served as backdrops to a number of student videos, including historical documentaries and fashion shows. En route to lunch, kindergarteners and first graders don't just walk single file through the blue-green waters of the Atlantis hallway; rather the whole class pretends to swim.

Beyond the overarching global motif, the infrastructure team had no formal plan; thus, it hoarded materials until a design theme presented itself. Parents had acquired the vast majority of materials through a combination of begging and scavenging. If team members walked by a store with a visual display they could imagine in the school, they would march right in and ask the visual manager if the school could have it when the store changed windows. Visual managers, even in the most exclusive stores, tend to be generous artistic types who hate to see their window displays end up in a landfill. Needless to say, parents developed a rather unorthodox approach to window-shopping.

Once the infrastructure team understood the natural retail market cycle, it had better luck securing donations. For instance, elaborate Christmas displays go up just after Halloween, but if parents were slow to pick up promised items after Christmas, they might very well be thrown away by New Year's Day. As reformers established relationships with visual managers, stores began to call the school to offer merchandise before it was scheduled to be thrown away. Co-op parents would immediately say, "Yes, yes, of course the school would love to have six life-size sheep!" And they would scoot right over and pick them up, even if they had no idea where their newly acquired flock might graze. If parents said they wanted a display item but were slow to pick it up, the store would not hold donations for them in the future. Creative reuse required quick response and an ample dose of faith. The Co-op soon realized it needed to identify a group of willing parents that had minivans or pickup trucks so that it could quickly mobilize when goods became available for pickup somewhere in the city.

If an establishment had lost its lease, the team would walk in and ask the manager if it could pick over the remains or clear out the store's infrastructure after its last day. If the owner said no (usually due to liability or lease constraints), the team would still return immediately after the store closed, when the demolition workers arrived. Most laborers were more than happy to let the parents cart stuff off their site. For example, after the hired demolition crew arrived to dismantle a closed neighborhood pharmacy, Nettelhorst's engineering staff and parent volunteers swooped in. Like an army of worker ants, the group carted out everything not bolted to the floor or walls. Using hand dollies, they wheeled it all down the block and right into the school, where the team transformed an empty classroom into a teacher-parent resource library. The demolition crew not only let the volunteers take anything of value, it even thanked them for making its job easier! Nettelhorst was in desperate need of everything; no doubt, whatever the parents could scrounge up would be put to use.

Sometimes the infrastructure team wanted something quite specific. For example, because Nettelhorst was an international magnet school, the team decided it wanted to hang globes on the ceiling for the length of the main hall. How might the team go about finding two hundred globes? A Google search uncovered Replogle Globes, a manufacturing plant in downstate Illinois whose owner was delighted to see his obsolete globes live in a school rather than a landfill (surely the charitable tax deduction would offset his shipping costs). The team learned that if it could reach a local manufacturer or supplier and wasn't particularly picky about what was donated, the school would often get lucky.

Susan was remarkably open to seeing existing spaces in a new light. For example, the school had always neglected the ground floor "garden level," assuming that students would naturally go upstairs to the office or to their classrooms. It had been so long since the building hosted families that the school rarely gave much thought to parents' needs. Neighborhood parents would be hard-pressed to navigate flights of stairs with children, coats, and strollers in hand. The solution was found at the end of a ramp just inside Nettelhorst's front door: a dilapidated teachers' lounge, cordoned off by institutional, tan burlap screens, with exposed pipes, crumbling walls, and a grimy kitchenette. While the sad room had served as the teachers' lunchroom for the past two decades, it had previously been the school's main kitchen for over a century. Why couldn't the space become a kitchen once again?

The infrastructure team set about transforming the old teacher's lunchroom into a French country kitchen where teachers might cook with students, parents could meet with teachers, or friends would stay to chat over a cup of coffee. Local merchants donated in-store kitchen displays, cabinets, and major appliances. The infrastructure team solicited pro bono architects to draw detailed plans to secure formal approval from CPS, which required that all plumbing and electrical work be performed to code by licensed professionals.

After the team stocked the new kitchen with donated equipment and supplies, Susan worried about theft and breakage. As she predicted, most of the fancy cookware walked within the first two years, negligent bakers broke the oven (which would then need to be replaced), and parents and teachers were reluctant to clean up after themselves. The Co-op was disheartened, but expected a certain degree of shrinkage and misuse. It replaced most of the items with comparable thrift store finds.

Susan was also concerned that parents might leave the kitchen and mill about the school unattended, taking the school's or someone else's property with them. Reformers countered that restaurants managed open coat racks by putting up a sign asking people not to leave their valuables and disavowing responsibility if items were lost or stolen. The school's security guard would likely catch a criminal if he tried to abscond with a computer monitor tucked under his coat or with someone else's child in tow. Increased parental presence might even decrease the chance for wrongdoing.[4]

On this front, the new community kitchen was wildly successful in bridging the home-school connection. After drop-off, parents would stay in the kitchen to drink a cup of coffee or nurse a baby, and then go upstairs to help shelve books in the library or to volunteer in their child's classroom. The kitchen put prospective parents at ease as soon as they entered the building. As parents hung up their coats and got situated, they discovered that their toddlers were quite content playing with a bead-maze table or the letter magnets on the refrigerator, just as comfortable as they were in their own home kitchen.

Most importantly, the new community kitchen benefitted the students. Suddenly, Nettelhorst teachers were cooking up a storm, and the students took the hands-on lessons to heart. In fact, one couple awoke one Sunday morning to find that their kindergartener had made them breakfast in bed: juice, toast, and a bowl of six raw eggs complete with broken shells, colored green. Her teacher had just read *Green Eggs and Ham* and then taught them how to make the dish themselves (of course, grown-ups would need to work the stove, the kindergartener knew; thus, mom and dad received their eggs raw). The new kitchen also allowed Nettelhorst to bring in chef Lois Levine's after-school culinary program; given the epidemic of child obesity in this country, the fact that Nettelhorst could offer cooking and nutritional education was particularly timely.[5] Lois's students would return home with recipes, knowledge, and stomachs filled with nutritious food, which for some would be their last meal until breakfast.

In turn, Nettelhorst's health and wellness initiative helped give mom Tracy Wozniak a toehold to launch a variety of green initiatives with parents and students, including school-wide recycling, composting, urban-container gardening, and healthy, locally sourced, organic after-school snacks.[6] The kitchen also provided several Chicago celebrity chefs, such as the Food Network's Hearty Boys, Dan Smith and Steve McDonagh, with a unique venue to offer master classes to lucky, wide-eyed (and wide-mouthed) Nettelhorst students.[7]

Nettelhorst's community kitchen became so integral to the school's new health and wellness curriculum and social life that it attracted the attention of Nate Berkus, nationally celebrated decorator, *New York Times* best-selling author, and featured design expert on *The Oprah Winfrey Show*. When supermoms Andrea Goldman and Kristen Engelman supervised the original kitchen transformation, they planned a light-use residential kitchen, not a high-use teaching kitchen for hundreds of children; six years of teacher lunches, parent coffees, and daily cooking classes had taken a toll. After touring the school, Nate was so impressed that the school community had worked so hard to spin gold out of straw that he decided to redesign and rebuild Nettelhorst's community kitchen, all pro bono.[8]

## ANGELS EVERYWHERE

Of course, the real credit for Nettelhorst's physical transformation should go to East Lakeview's incredible generosity, which amounted to over a half-million dollars in goods and services. Remarkably, most donations did not come from big corporations, but from small independent companies that did not have pro bono budgets or formal community service missions. Managers of local paint stores, especially Joshua Goldmeier at Sappanos and Jim Boisvert at Sherwin-Williams, not only donated enough paint for the entire school, but also gave the parents potential leads for professionals to apply it. Professional painters adopted classrooms, working off the clock at night or on weekends. When parents called painters and contractors to ask for help, some may have accepted because they hoped the store would refer paying business to them in the future, but most just wanted to help because they thought it was the right thing to do.

Virtually every inch of the school tells a story of an individual's kindness and generosity. For example, when the infrastructure team asked Oscar Jurados, the owner of a small local painting company, to adopt one of three hallways for the new community school, he offered to paint all three hallways and the stairwell. It was a huge job, one that would take three men using paint sprayers more than a week. When asked why he was being so incredibly generous, Oscar told the story about when an earthquake destroyed his Mexican village. With great fanfare, a rich man from a neighboring town came to help the victims, offering a truck-full of old clothing for the families of this devastated village. As a young boy, Oscar vowed that if he ever attained the American dream, if someone in need came to him for help, he would answer the call in a way that was genuinely helpful. Nettelhorst is filled with similar stories of how community members came together to rebuild their neighborhood public school.

Beyond individual craftsmen and merchants, strangers mysteriously appeared to lend a hand. For example, when a fancy linen store closed its downtown location, the manager donated a beautiful, zinc-topped, oak counter to the school. When the pro bono movers arrived, they were sad to report that the hulking piece would have to stay in their truck because it required at least ten men to lift it up the stairs to the library. Just as the parents went outside to say goodbye to their new circulation desk, ten young men who were leaving the corner coffee shop walked over to see what all the fuss was about. Sure enough, the men offered to help move the counter up the two flights of stairs. After a solid hour of laboring over the bulky piece, the ten exhausted men stood over a public school's new circulation desk, and even thanked the school for giving them the opportunity to help!

Like Tom Sawyer, parent volunteers would solicit neighbors who were just causally walking by the school. A promise to lend a hand for just a couple of minutes often turned into several hours of intense labor. For instance, as an end-of-year activity, Nettelhorst students had tied strips of cloth onto the playground fence as a symbol of their gratitude and good intentions for the universe. All summer long, the rainbow fence displayed an undulating sea of colorful fabric. Come Labor Day weekend, co-op moms began the tedious project of removing all the weathered, tangled ribbons so that the school year could begin with a fresh new look. By the end of the summer evening, the moms had dozens of strangers—in various states of sobriety—assisting them.

Why did so many strangers offer to help? Many neighbors certainly volunteered their time because they liked kids and believed that public school was a worthy cause. But mostly, co-op volunteers had an infectious enthusiasm that was hard for curious neighbors to resist. It also didn't hurt that their "work" projects were intriguing; how often is one asked to hand a disco ball to a stranger halfway up a tree? When curious neighbors would walk by a volunteer gardening project and discover that the woman, dressed in a sweatshirt and holding the shovel, was none other than the school's principal, it was hard not to be inspired.

Reformers needed to improve Nettelhorst's infrastructure sufficiently in order to compel neighborhood parents to give the school a second look, but their efforts achieved so much more. Despite the work of so many professional artists, the school is not a static stage set but a constantly evolving, dynamic learning environment. The energy in the hallways is palpable. Although Susan and the Co-op would still need to convince prospective parents that Nettelhorst offered more than a pretty paint job, at the very least curious parents could now find their way to the school's front door, and once inside, would be comfortable enough to stay and listen to the pitch.

# THREE

# SUPPORT SYSTEMS

## CONTRACT SERVICES

I F REFORMERS were ever going to dig Nettelhorst out of its hole, they desperately needed to leverage every ounce of the school's limited power and develop strategic partnerships. Reformers thought strategically about what the school could possibly offer the marketplace. Nettelhorst *could* offer space in a densely packed urban setting, market access to students and potentially to neighborhood families, and a possibility for media exposure. Nettelhorst *could not* offer much in the way of capital, supervision, support services, oversight, or security. With these two assumptions in place, Nettelhorst looked beyond the traditional schoolhouse model...

### SPECIAL EVENTS

While most people might look at Nettelhorst's two shabby playgrounds as a study in urban blight, the special events team saw gold. Reformers imagined that the playgrounds, though not ideal for children, could be spectacular venues for community events. The school offered an enormous facility situated in a vibrant neighborhood with substantial car and foot traffic. Although the school offered limited parking, it was close to public transportation. The school just needed some help making connections.

While Nettelhorst already enjoyed a cordial relationship with the Lakeview East Chamber of Commerce, reformers worked to forge a more dynamic partnership. Maureen Martino, the executive director of the Lakeview East Chamber of Commerce, keenly understood the symbiotic relationships between a viable public school, increased property values, and happy neighborhood merchants. She logged hundreds of hours with Nettelhorst moms Stephanie Schrodt, Jennifer Howell, Janet Peterson, and Melanie Glick planning elaborate holiday events for the community. In the first year of the strengthened partnership, the chamber hosted several neighborhood events at the school, including a "Halloween Hoopla" complete with horse-drawn hayrides, a "Little Bunny Egg Hunt," and a "Pet Fest" with pony rides and a petting zoo. Although the special events team worked tirelessly to ensure that community events were successful, the chamber's influence allowed the team to host events that were far more elaborate than anything the school could ever have produced solo.

The special events team also helped the chamber plan and market these events. Pro bono graphic designers created whimsical, event-specific postcards and posters that the chamber printed by the thousands. Co-op volunteers hand-delivered stacks of event postcards to neighborhood businesses, churches, synagogues, and parks.

Amazingly, local private and parochial schools also agreed to distribute chamber postcards to their own families. While most schools would never dream of handing out another school's promotional materials, the idea that Nettelhorst—poor, pathetic Nettelhorst—was audacious enough to think it could poach their students was a joke. And yet, chamber event postcards allowed the Co-op to extend subtle "school admission" invitations to private and parochial school parents, personally delivered by their own children. While reformers didn't expect any of these families to switch schools midstream, a positive experience at a Nettelhorst event might lead them to question their sanity for writing all those fat checks, if only the tiniest bit. If Nettelhorst could insert itself into the public/private school dialogue, it might become a choice for their younger children or even children of their current friends. Reformers hoped that well-produced chamber events would give the school desperately needed credibility and help spark this initial conversation.

Although the school publicly thanked the chamber throughout community events, most neighbors mistakenly believed that the Co-op deserved all the credit for hosting them. It was only natural: co-op parents formed the army that distributed the event's postcards and staffed the events—from manning the craft and sign-in tables to making raffle announcements to running the popcorn machine. Although the Co-op helped the chamber tailor events to appeal to neighborhood parents, it never could have financed or executed anything as elaborate as what the chamber delivered. The misperception allowed the school to look far more solid than it actually was.

However, the team did such a good job marketing the events that the planners found themselves overwhelmed and unprepared. For example, at the Halloween Hoopla, the chamber's first community event at Nettelhorst, hundreds of pint-sized neighborhood ghosts and goblins descended on the school. The devil was in the details: How were planners to know that the actual length of the hayride around the neighborhood was fairly inconsequential to a six-year-old, but a wait time of more than ten minutes seemed like an eternity? Or that numbered wristbands would allow everyone to enjoy the party rather than wait in a long queue for the Clydesdales to clip-clop back to school? Or that having toddlers bob for apples in the cold was a recipe for disaster? Or that the failure to list an age cap on the postcard meant that some very scary revelers would show up?

After the first Halloween Hoopla, planners faced a steep learning curve. Clearly, parties needed double or triple the number of volunteers and careful, creative planning to control crowds and manage expectations. Come spring, the team thought it was ready, but despite all the hard lessons learned at the first event, the first Little Bunny Egg Hunt was a nightmare. The flimsy yellow police tape was hardly sufficient to hold back the frenzied horde waiting for the right moment to attack the hay-strewn parking lot. Volunteers looked on in utter horror as older kids trampled over younger children while their parents seemed to cheer them on. In the midst of the melee, desperate parents shouted for missing toddlers. Lesson learned: Families needed to register their children at the front gate, where volunteers distributed numbered wristbands, color-coded by age group (yellow for 3–5 year-olds, blue for 6–8 year olds, and red for 9–12 year-olds). Organizers called staggered age groups for three distinct, stampede-free egg hunts. As soon as participants found a plastic egg, they could hop over to the other side of the playground and redeem it for a merchant-donated gift basket. Moving forward: one age group; one egg; one prize; no tears.

Through trial and error, reformers discovered what kinds of special events the school could achieve successfully and what kinds it couldn't. The school stumbled when it tried to host events that didn't coincide with traditional family holidays. Whereas neighborhood parents needed to find fun activities to do with their children on Halloween and Easter, the chamber's Pet Fest and the local bank's Safety Day required elaborate explanation. When the school tried to convince people to come to a manufactured event, it needed to sell the venue *and* the concept *and* hope that the guests remembered it on the right date. Even though the families that attended Pet Fest or Safety Day had a good time, event planners were more than a little disappointed by the low turnout.

In another example, a month of Sunday evening summer dances in the school's front playlot crashed and burned. Convinced it would be a smash hit like the city's popular outdoor summer dance program, co-op parents commissioned Big City Swing Dance to provide an hour of professional dance lessons followed by an evening of dancing to a DJ for a mere five-dollar entrance fee. The Co-op was undaunted when the chamber took a pass on hosting the month-long series; if just twenty couples came to dance each Sunday, planners could cover their costs. Attendance couldn't have been worse. Few Nettelhorst parents were around over the summer, and even fewer husbands wanted to hire a sitter to swing dance as the general public paraded by. Neighbors appeared amused but hardly enticed. Even after volunteers dropped the entrance fee and hawked postcards on the street, adults were reluctant to join in without a cocktail, a date, a proper venue, or at least a critical mass. No doubt, the handful of dancing couples on the playlot had a great time, but the evening never really felt like the party that the planners had envisioned.

From these ill-conceived events, reformers learned four valuable lessons:

- The Co-op lacked the resources to be the sole sponsor of community events.
- The school needed to stick with a few tried-and-true, child-centered, holiday events.
- The school couldn't provide the social comforts that adults seemed to require to really cut loose.
- By summer, school volunteers were tapped out.

These four lessons offered one notable exception:

- Nettelhorst could be a great venue if a third party wanted to host an adult-centered event that was strategically aligned with the reform movement's mission.

For example, in October, Nettelhorst's playlot becomes the scene of a raucous party during the Chicago Marathon. As the official Mile 8 water station, neighborhood clubs erect platforms for DJs and go-go dancers in drag to cheer on the runners. Scores of volunteers come to distribute water and sports drinks, but the party takes place whether Nettelhorst families actually show up or not. Similarly, Nettelhorst is also on the route for Chicago's annual Gay and Lesbian Pride Parade, and while the front playlot is usually quite festive, it is not the school's responsibility to deliver fifty thousand happy revelers to Nettelhorst's front door. Reformers learned that the school could become a valued partner to the community simply by playing host to the neighborhood's party.

## FARMERS' MARKET

Reformers also imagined that Nettelhorst's asphalt-covered front playground would be a great venue for a farmers' market. East Lakeview had been clamoring for a farmers' market for years, and reformers felt confident that their corner's substantial car and foot traffic could support one. Susan was keen to host a market, but obviously, the school did not have the time, energy, or expertise to manage one. When co-op parents heard through the grapevine that Bensidoun USA, a business that manages most of the farmers' markets in France, wanted to expand operations to Chicago, e-mails began flying across the Atlantic. The Nettelhorst French Market, which offered select merchandise in addition to flowers and produce, seemed an ideal partner—the company provided all the equipment, marketing, insurance, and management.[1] All the school needed to provide was a location for the market (which otherwise sat empty on the weekend). Because planners didn't expect the farmers' market to open a new a funding stream for the school, the deal seemed like a slam dunk.

However, co-op parents had no idea that starting a new farmers' market, even a market entirely contracted out to a third party, would be so complicated. First, the school needed to get approval from the CPS real estate department. Even though other schools hosted markets and fairs, the Nettelhorst French Market needed to permanently install special metal fasteners in the playground's asphalt to hold up its tents. CPS needed to determine how the scores of little holes in the ground would affect liability issues, maintenance, and aesthetics.

Second, the school needed to secure a green light from the alderman. Because reformers had already forged a relationship with the current alderman, Tom Tunney, when Jacqueline arrived at his office with a pipe dream of a farmers' market, he immediately picked up the phone and called the presidents of the various neighborhood groups and the Chamber of Commerce to ask for their opinions and support of the project. Even with the alderman's backing, the school would still need to answer questions concerning garbage, trucks, parking, security, and safety.

In light of all these deal breakers, the school was exceedingly lucky to find park parent Taylor Galyean, a gifted architect/urban planner, to help shepherd the project through city hall.

Before sinking thousands of dollars of nonrecoverable infrastructure into the school's asphalt playground, Bensidoun USA wanted guarantees that the mayor's office would renew market permits annually and fix the rate of taxes and fees, in writing. The city of Chicago had a very different concept: If a French company wanted to launch an untried, mixed-use market concept within a densely populated neighborhood, Bensidoun USA was not in the driver's seat.

The mayor's office, the ward alderman, and the fire marshal acted as the holy trinity of urban planning. If Bensidoun USA did a good job, the market could stay; if it did a poor job, the market would be shut down—immediately. And the city of Chicago made clear that *mais non*, it didn't put things in writing. Period. Needless to say, even though co-op parents were desperate to bring the market to their little corner of the world, they had their hands full trying to navigate the Gallic–American cultural divide.

Beyond logistical and cultural complications, some neighbors and merchants were less than thrilled when the news of the market opening became public. The local alderman fielded complaints from residents about parking and congestion. The school absorbed tirades from neighboring merchants, particularly small corner grocers, knickknack shops, and bucket florists, who feared that a farmers' market would threaten their business (one florist personally saw fit to deliver a bouquet, accompanied by a diatribe, to Jacqueline's house). While the chamber looked forward to increased foot traffic in the neighborhood, it worried that its small business owners, who were already strained by skyrocketing rents, might be hit hard. Bensidoun USA tried to appease the chamber by offering neighborhood merchants first dibs on renting market stalls, but even at the daily rate of just thirty dollars a table, not one responded.

In the end, the naysayers came to appreciate the added value that the farmers' market brought to East Lakeview, but the project never would have gotten off the ground had the co-op team sought consensus from the neighborhood at large. Reformers learned that city planning is not for the fainthearted. The school got a green light to develop the market from key stakeholders—the city, the alderman, the school board, and the presidents of the two neighborhood associations—and trusted that everyone else would come on board after tasting the season's first heirloom tomato.

At just seventeen stalls, Nettelhorst's French Market was too small to generate much revenue for the school, but it did help put Nettelhorst on the map. Suddenly, community members—including people who didn't have children—had a reason to come to Nettelhorst, a phenomenon that hadn't occurred in over thirty years. With very little work on the school's end, the weekly farmers' market became something of a fabled town square: Merchants sold their wares, musicians played, spas gave free massages, big kids painted faces, and little kids sold lemonade. Every Saturday, the Co-op would distribute promotional information to a captive audience, and Susan would offer a private tour of the school to anyone who showed even the slightest interest.

## COMMUNITY SCHOOL

As the co-op's special events team was spinning Nettelhorst's straw into gold, the enrichment team needed to do the same. The team faced a real challenge: How could the school lasso arts, culture, and sports when it had absolutely no financial resources? Then the team remembered that mythical Italian village the neighboring principal had spoken of so fondly, where the cobblers and the bakers and the mamas all pitched in to educate the village. Could this idyllic Reggio Emilia model transmute into a new paradigm for Nettelhorst?

The team imagined an enrichment program called 4+1=! The basic idea was that everyone in the community had something valuable to offer Nettelhorst students. From the neighborhood dry cleaner to the restaurant line cook, everyone would be welcome to come in and teach. In reality, the team wasn't sure how this plan might work. Was the tailor supposed to come in and show kids how to sew buttons? Did he need a lesson plan? A criminal background check? A TB shot? And how would students get to his shop? What would they do there? Mend trousers? It was a noble idea, but if getting the farmers' market proved any indication, reformers would need to come up with a more tenable plan if the Italian village concept was going to translate.

In the course of research, the team found a website called Schools Without Walls, which listed some of the finest cultural institutions throughout the city that offered free programming for public schools. All a school had to do was contact the organization and register, simple as that. The program, funded in part by CPS, provided a framework for field trips and offered in-school programming by Chicago's most venerable cultural organizations. Who knew that public schools had so many amazing resources at their disposal? If stellar enrichment experiences were so readily available, reformers wondered why Nettelhorst wasn't lighting up like a Christmas tree. Was it possible that the school had weighed the logistical and financial demands of going to the museum or the symphony and actually decided it was a better idea to stay home? Well, the team decided, if Mohammed won't go to the mountain, the mountain must come to Mohammed! If it was too logistically challenging for Nettelhorst to take advantage of the city, perhaps cultural institutions might be willing to take their shows on the road, not just for a special day or a short-term program, but permanently.

Inspired by the Schools Without Walls program, the enrichment team envisioned what its neighborhood school might look like if Chicago's best cultural purveyors for children had an enduring presence in the building. The team brainstormed the most outlandish possibilities. Wouldn't it be funny if Old Town School of Folk Music taught music classes at Nettelhorst? Or what if Fairytale Ballet taught dance? Maybe Lill Street Art Center could come in and teach art? And H. M. D. Academy could offer tae kwon do? What if Emerald City directed the third-grade play? The enrichment team thought it had hit the jackpot—it would seek out the best cultural institutions in the city and ask if they might like to directly partner with Nettelhorst.

It wasn't so much that the park parents believed that their precious children needed to have the very best of everything or that they needed to have every available minute devoted to an adult-supervised enrichment activity. The reality of urban living meant that the halcyon days of unsupervised playtime after school—the kind where children scampered from house to house eating snacks, or frolicking outside until dinnertime—was a nostalgic relic. In truth, most neighborhood kids under the age of thirteen would never be outside their house without some kind of adult chaperone. Given safety concerns, Chicago's long winter, and limited private indoor and outdoor space, even if nonworking parents desired afternoons of unstructured free-play and exploration for their children, most still needed a school-based aftercare program. If Nettelhorst could manage to contract all of its after-school activities from respected purveyors, prospective parents would surely take a second look at their neighborhood school.

Of course, the next question the team would need to answer would be from the partner's perspective. Why would a cultural institution choose to partner with a school it had never heard of before, or if it had heard of the school, believed it was terrible? What benefit could an underperforming, underutilized public school possibly offer an established cultural institution? The enrichment team began to form its response. In all likelihood, an institution's mission already included children's outreach, and very likely public school outreach, as well. A satellite operation could honor the partner's mission and broaden its reach by extending access to both Nettelhorst students and neighborhood children. The school had plenty of space; it was located in an artsy, vibrant neighborhood with significant foot traffic; public transportation was a few convenient steps from Nettelhorst's front door. The idea of satellite classes wasn't so outlandish.

Reformers worked from the assumption that the relationship needed to be mutually beneficial. Partners could teach their regular classes at Nettelhorst while enjoying free rent, marketing, and utilities. Partners would charge students their usual rates and could cancel any class that didn't meet their self-determined minimum enrollment.

Hence, businesses could expand without incurring any additional risk or overhead.

Reformers would ask partners for only two things in return. One, partners had to offer scholarships to Nettelhorst students (which they routinely did, anyway). Two, partners had to contribute a nominal amount (to be mutually determined) to the school's regular curricular day. As much as Nettelhorst needed money, it needed expertise more. Reformers figured that no matter how successful the school became, it was never going to have the resources to hire Lilly the ceramist, Peggy the ballerina, or Skippy the yacht boy to teach classes dedicated to their crafts—this was a way to bring experts into the school without relying on external funding. The partnership would be a win-win situation.

As soon as the first big-name cultural institution, Old Town School of Folk Music, partnered with Nettelhorst, others quickly jumped on the proverbial bandwagon. After all, if such a respected institution was not afraid that a puny, mismanaged satellite program would tarnish its reputation, what did anyone else have to fear? Surely all the partners figured that they could bail out if the partnership seemed disastrous.[2]

With Nettelhorst's "sizzle package" of stellar cultural partners in place, it quickly became clear that the school had bitten off more than it could chew. This untested fee-for-service community school model would need far more oversight than what the co-op's volunteers or the school's administration could muster. So the enrichment team sought out a not-for-profit managing partner for the new, in-school community center and its thirteen partners.

In a twist of fate, Jane Addams Hull House Association (Hull House), one of Chicago's oldest and largest not-for-profit social service agencies, was in the process of moving its nearby community center to follow its core constituency farther north. While some neighbors celebrated the move, most were saddened to be losing ceramics, photography, swimming, and child care. The Co-op finally had something of a clear assignment for the alderman: Encourage Hull House to manage a fee-for-service community center *from within Nettelhorst*, utilizing the school's newly minted cultural partners. No one had any idea how this fee-for-service enterprise would work in reality, but there didn't seem to be much downside since no one would be risking any capital. Hull House would still sell off its crumbling building to developers and use the proceeds to open its new North Side center as planned, but thanks to the innovative Nettelhorst partnership, the venerable agency could still service East Lakeview.

Hull House decided to take the risk and partner with Nettelhorst. No sooner had it signed on to manage this untried in-school community center than reformers learned of a new grant offering from the Community Schools Initiative. CPS was selecting six schools to pilot a new program that extended the school day with expanded enrichment opportunities. In the published Request for Proposal (RFP), individual schools would partner with a not-for-profit agency that would administer programming and services. The grant offered $300,000 over three years (with financial support split between CPS and private foundations) to run a community center within a school. Nettelhorst already had a community school model that was hand-off ready! If Nettelhorst won this grant, the enrichment team would have the legitimacy and the seed money it needed to get its on-paper community center off the ground.

As much as Nettelhorst and Hull House believed themselves to be the perfect candidates, and as much as Susan and the reformers believed themselves to be the ideal advocates, the school was hardly a shoo-in. The Community Schools Initiative targeted underperforming schools in low-income areas; Nettelhorst met the low-income requirement, with over 70 percent of its students falling below the poverty line, but it was still better off than many CPS schools. Only 35 percent of Nettelhorst students tested at or above grade level, but here again, that figure was superior to many CPS schools that were on academic probation. Moreover, the RFP said nothing about a fee-for-service model. Why should CPS and the mayor choose Nettelhorst?

To give itself every possible edge, Nettelhorst resolved to enlist the assistance of its local politicians. Jacqueline and Nicole felt that if they could just speak with someone in the mayor's office, they could make a compelling argument in favor of the Nettelhorst model. Thanks to the extraordinary persistence of their state representative, Sara Feigenholtz, the women landed their important meeting downtown. Jacqueline and Nicole contended that Nettelhorst might not have been the school that the Community Schools Initiative had in mind when it wrote the RFP, but it should have been; *all* children, including middle-class children, deserved enrichment opportunities in public school. The Parents' Co-op had already done such a phenomenal job of mobilizing the community in just a few months—imagine how high the school could fly if given some kind of formal backing and financial support. Thanks in large part to the efforts of Roscoe Park mom Eileen Swartout, who helped write the grant, Nettelhorst and Hull House submitted a persuasive application to help seal the deal. When Nettelhorst became one of Chicago's six inaugural community schools, the earth stopped spinning. The school finally had a legitimate way to absorb all the goodness that might come from the larger community.

However, bringing the community school to life was more challenging than anyone imagined. Nettelhorst was pioneering a fee-for-service community school model, and like almost every other scheme the reformers tried to hatch, transforming the dream into a reality was a bracing endeavor. The parties had countless mind-numbing logistical issues to navigate. How would new programming affect the school's existing state-funded, before- and after-school programs? How would the school handle issues of liability? How would its partners contribute to the curriculum? How would the partners determine the criteria for scholarships? Who would collect fees, and how would they be processed? How much autonomy would partners have to set their own rates, schedules, and class sizes? Would the school trump the partners' obligations, or vice versa? What if a partner proved to be a bad fit? And then there were questions about service and supervision, such as janitorial and clerical needs, security, and general oversight. Was the principal supposed to be on call all day and evening? Like Fantasia's regenerating brooms, every solution only spawned more and more questions.

The outside consultants hired by CPS to facilitate the grant for the six inaugural schools struggled to reconcile its stated protocol with the reality that already existed on the ground. In the first year of the grant, pilot schools were supposed to develop a working oversight committee of community stakeholders who would then target a list of potential partners. Nettelhorst already had a list of committed partners solicited by stakeholders who had no interaction with anyone inside the school besides the principal. Consultants challenged reformers to bring the school's teachers and parents to the table, when the Co-op knew full well that such inclusion would likely imperil the movement. Reformers simply couldn't afford a year of brainstorming sessions and coalition building to get their community center off the ground. Nettelhorst had promised neighborhood families that the "sizzle package" of cultural partners would begin its programming by the time their children enrolled for kindergarten in September.

To complicate matters further, the consultants feared that the new partners, as respected as they were, did not really intend to serve the needs of Nettelhorst's current population. The reformers, who had worked so hard to develop a self-sustaining model, were frustrated by this charge. While Nettelhorst's students no longer took school buses home at three o'clock, they still needed to trek across town, and few chose to remain on the property following classes for any reason. The reformers argued that the school's pre-existing, free after-school programming had been underutilized, so why shouldn't partners offer their services to neighborhood children who desired them? If the current students could not afford the partners' customary rates, everyone had agreed to offer generous scholarships. If students could not, or would not, stay after school, they would still benefit since all the partners had committed to contributing to the regular curriculum day. The fee-for-service model accepted the fact that all the community school partners, however enlightened, weren't running charities.

The consultants were adamant that the grant had been given to Nettelhorst in its current form and existence—not the pie-in-the-sky fantasy of what Nettelhorst might someday become. As such, the consultants maintained that, first and foremost, the new community school needed to serve the current school population. Reformers found themselves staring down Alice's rabbit hole: The school desperately needed the expertise and reputation of the chosen cultural partners if it hoped to draw middle-class families. If the community center did not open on time, as promised, neighborhood families would surely lose faith that Nettelhorst could deliver on any other front. If neighborhood families failed to return en masse, CPS was threatening to close Nettelhorst as a whole, a move that would hardly benefit the school's current students and teachers, or the community at large.

Nevertheless, the consultants had a point. Dangling fancy extracurricular activities in front of children who lacked the means to take advantage of them was offensive in the extreme. Every answer seemed to have an equally valid counterpoint, but reformers knew one thing for certain: *The school simply had to move forward.*

The compressed time frame added pressure to an already strained marriage. Hull House and Nettelhorst struggled to reconcile their competing visions for the partnership with the new reality that was unfolding. Since 1889, Jane Addams's core mission was to serve Chicago's underserved and underprivileged, but Nettelhorst's current reforms weren't going to benefit everyone equally. Emotions ran high as parties confronted thinly veiled charges of racism, classism, hubris, and incompetence. Even the eternally positive consultants began to sour as the parties struggled to transcend politics and ideologies. To everyone's credit, all parties tenaciously worked through their differences behind closed doors until they found common ground.

The waters ahead were uncharted. How could Nettelhorst engage disinterested students or absentee parents? How could Hull House remain true to its founder's vision while serving both the privileged and the underprivileged? How could funders accept a governing body of stakeholders that wasn't diverse, inclusive, or even legitimately invested? How could the administration run a community center when it was working overtime to run a school? How could partners be expected to hire instructors or promote classes when they had no idea when, or if, the community center was going to open? How could reformers deliver a five-year game plan when they didn't even have a strategy for the next five minutes? Thankfully, a

Roscoe Park mom, Suzanne Poland Noetzel, came to the school's rescue, working twenty-four/seven to hammer out the first Jane's Place schedule. In fewer than ten months, Jane Addams Hull House Association and Nettelhorst miraculously opened their innovative community school partnership, Jane's Place at Nettelhorst, on time, as promised.

To mark the occasion, Nettelhorst planned an all-school assembly, inviting recent donors, local politicians, and Jane's Place's new cultural partners. Everyone was enthusiastic: Hull House reaffirmed its commitment to the Lakeview community, politicians spoke about school reform, Nicole thanked donors for investing in the dream, and Jacqueline vowed that partners would offer chess, Latin, tap dancing, or anything the students could dream up. Jane's Place at Nettelhorst would be *their* community school.

While the powers that be congratulated each other on a successful unveiling, Jacqueline and Nicole were shaken. The park parents certainly had much to celebrate: In fewer than nine months, they had taken the pulse of the neighborhood, navigated the school's complex political climate, and partnered with some of the city's most respected enrichment providers for a innovative, fee-for-service community school, a model that very well might hold the key to turning around the school. And yet, up until that morning, the cofounders had never seen the entire school population assembled, and simply assumed that everyone would fall madly in love with Jane's Place at its coming-out party. While Nettelhorst students did cheer enthusiastically for an appropriately attired ballerina, sailor, martial arts expert, and so on, they seemed to have very little understanding what all the excitement actually meant. Worse yet, the teachers, stationed every few rows to maintain order, seemed utterly nonplussed by all the fuss. What if the teachers never came to appreciate the finely wrapped present that so many concerned parties had delivered to their front door? What if the current students never had any interest in availing themselves of any of Jane's Place's fine enrichment classes? What if Susan had oversold herself, and the school had bitten off more than it could possibly chew?

And just as the co-op reformers feared, the challenges of designing and opening a community school were quickly eclipsed by the challenges of actually running one. Everyone expected that Jane's Place would experience some start-up pains, but the way in which it originated led to a unique set of seemingly unavoidable difficulties. Susan believed that Jane's Place would be a self-sufficient, deferential appendage to the school; funders, on the other hand, expected that Nettelhorst would *become* a community school, with the school and the not-for-profit agency sharing power, authority, and resources. The funders fully expected Nettelhorst and Hull House to work together to forge a true partnership with a shared vision.

Reformers imagined yet a different concept. Neighborhood parents had concocted their innovative, fee-for-service model around the park sandbox; it was only a stroke of luck that the community school's grant materialized to give their plan wings. Reformers expected to get Jane's Place off paper by following the same take-no-prisoners tactics that other co-op teams utilized to quickly accomplish their goals—namely, to bulldoze through and assuage, sidestep, or neutralize all potential opposition. When—and if—the rest of Nettelhorst's stakeholders, whatever their mood, came around to the idea, Jane's Place would be up and running, at which point it would be in a position to tweak the offerings to accommodate various interests. If the powers that be could not understand the series of steps that brought the community school to fruition, reformers were at a loss.

As the funders dictated terms, reformers could barely contain their frustration. The funders were willing to overlook the fact that Nettelhorst's novel concept was hatched in a vacuum, but the grant mandated that the school assemble a diverse board of stakeholders for an oversight committee. Parent reformers, who had already studied the neighborhood market in depth, did not have the patience to bring any Johnny-come-latelies up to speed; there was simply too much work that still needed to be done. Moreover, they feared that widening the circle would only invite the school's disenfranchised factions to sabotage their efforts. In time, reformers believed that the oversight committee would evolve organically, but to force the issue in the early stages was just asking for trouble. Nevertheless, the threat of losing funding was a powerful incentive to at least appear more open-minded.

In contrast, both Susan and Hull House genuinely believed that diverse viewpoints on the oversight committee would ultimately lead to increased consensus from the greater school community. They tried multiple tactics to encourage different constituencies to join the committee: They distributed bilingual flyers, newsletters, and surveys; asked teachers to phone parents; staffed informational tables on report card pick-up days; and blanketed the neighborhood with posters. Despite all their efforts, Jane's Place had little success recruiting or maintaining new members for the board. Susan finally decided to solve the "diversity problem" by coercing the same handful of parents and teachers who were already serving on other Nettelhorst volunteer committees (LSC, Friends of Nettelhorst, neighborhood tutors, and Parents' Co-op) to make time for yet another "essential" meeting.

While this familiar cast of loyal teachers and die-hard co-op volunteers knew that they couldn't say no, Nettelhorst's handful of community school partners weren't playing that game. Partners had their own businesses to run; they had neither the time nor the energy to drone on about what Nettelhorst students needed or wanted. They had agreed to teach off-site classes at Nettelhorst because reformers promised to maximize their profits and exposure and minimize their risks and hassles. It should have been no surprise that the partners skipped most Jane's Place meetings, leaving the same dozen people to slog through pointless brainstorming sessions about what was going wrong.

And a great deal *was* going wrong. The rush to open the community center on time meant that reformers and Hull House employees had frantically cobbled together a schedule without any clear insight into the mechanics of the regular school day or CPS calendar. Teachers had little understanding of the new community school beyond the fact that the administration was asking them to work after school for less pay (one of the many unexpected consequences of accepting new funding). The phones were ringing off the hook, but the office staff had no idea how to respond to Jane's Place queries. The maintenance staff was complaining to the building engineer about the extra work required to set up for more activities and clean up after more people. The students were questioning what Jane's Place could possibly offer them since most children needed to begin the long trek home via public transportation immediately after school if they hoped to arrive before dinner. On the day enrichment classes were scheduled to begin, Jane's Place still had no formal mechanism in place to register students, process class fees, or award scholarships. The hastily hired resource coordinator didn't even have a working phone line or computer. The same problems that dogged Nettelhorst as a school seemed magnified with all the added pressure of managing the new community center.

The only Jane's Place partnership that wasn't going terribly awry was the relationship with the Jewish Community Center (JCC). While Hull House was the managing partner for the new community school, the JCC was Nettelhorst's on-site aftercare provider. Nettelhorst students (except preschoolers) could go to the JCC Kids' Klub immediately following the school day or after Jane's Place classes; there they could eat snacks, do art projects, play games, or just get a head start on their homework. Parents could register children for every weekday afternoon or just certain days. If parents bought a prepaid "flex card," they could call the office anytime before the end of the regular school day to get Kids' Klub coverage that same afternoon. Because the JCC handled all its own registration and finances, it avoided many of the start-up headaches that afflicted other Jane's Place partners.

Although many of the logistics worked well with the JCC partnership, it also had its share of issues. Who was responsible for furnishing or cleaning the Kids' Klub rooms? How would the JCC handle disruptive students? Who would supervise students going from Kids' Klub to Jane's Place classes and back again? How could parents reach JCC counselors when so many calls fell into Nettelhorst's perpetual voice mail hell? As the front doorbell rang only in the tuition-based preschool after three o'clock, did the JCC expect the TBP teachers to buzz in a relentless wave of Kids' Klub parents all afternoon? Although the JCC, like all Jane's Place partners, carried its own liability insurance, who was really responsible when a Kids' Klub child was somewhere other than Kids' Klub? What if partners were late to pick up their kids? What if parents were late to pick up their child or were financially delinquent? As the JCC closed for Jewish holidays, what would happen to Nettelhorst students who still needed aftercare on these days? The school needed to address all these technical problems, as well.

Although all the Jane's Place partners, including the JCC, had well-deserved reputations that might only be undone by a willful act of sabotage, everyone was more than a little irritated by the new community school's slipshod operation. While the partners were enthusiastic about joining the project initially, by the time Jane's Place officially opened for business, Nettelhorst's rah-rah spirit and endearing incompetence had worn thin. Less than a year into the grant, most partners had reached their threshold of tolerance, and several key partners were threatening to pull out altogether if the school couldn't shape up and deliver on its promises.

The partners' expectations for the new community school hardly seemed outrageous. Established institutions set their schedules months in advance and need generous lead times to hire teachers and coordinate programs. Partners needed to know how many students to expect, how many scholarships would be required, and when and where classes would meet. Classrooms needed to be clean and available when the instructors arrived. While all partners needed to pay their own instructors for teaching at Nettelhorst, Hull House acted as the financial clearinghouse. The job was straightforward enough: collect tuition for each afterschool program (except for the JCC Kids' Klub), process the checks, and then return these fees in a lump sum to the various providers. Partners fully expected to receive payments in a timely manner.

If Jane's Place hoped to open for a second semester, it needed to quickly improve the program's management. The oversight committee had a steep learning curve: from scheduling classes, to setting class fees and scholarships, to navigating in-school contributions and existing conflicts. At every turn, the school feverishly managed logistical and pedagogical decisions. If a rescheduled eighth-grade basketball game suddenly conflicted with a tae kwon do class, who got the gym? If a scholarship student missed numerous classes, could a partner unregister him from the program? Who would be responsible for children if parents were late? If a partner wanted to kick a disruptive student out of a class, where would the child wait until his parents arrived? If a room was a mess, who was supposed to clean it up? Who was responsible for making sure the front door was open? Closed? Locked? Everyone was getting cranky. Reformers were beginning to wonder if winning the grant was such a godsend after all.

As the school maneuvered through these start-up issues, five guiding principles emerged: First and foremost, *Nettelhorst was a public elementary school that needed to serve its own students*. Even though Jane's Place intended to welcome all children—regardless of where they attended school—when push came to shove, Nettelhorst students would have first dibs on filling classes and first priority on space. So if the school rescheduled its basketball game and needed to commandeer the gym, the tae kwon do students might need to make do in the lunchroom. Understandably, the instructor wouldn't be happy about it, but he needed to be flexible. The flip side to this advantage was that Nettelhorst needed to shoulder more responsibility than the not-for-profit partner or contract partners for the care of children under its roof. The added frustrations of increased security, liability, and maintenance were part of the bargain.

Second, *Nettelhorst students needed to show as much respect to the community school partners as they would to their regular teachers*. Partners could demand that Nettelhorst students (and parents) show the same level of discipline, effort, and consideration as their own in-house students, and follow their standard procedures if their expectations were not met. Participation in Jane's Place programming was not a right but a privilege. However, partners needed to spell out their expectations more clearly and more frequently than they might need to with their usual clientele to avoid misunderstandings.

Third, *the school needed to respect partners by being professional*. The school could still improvise, but it needed to become less reactive. It needed to come to terms with the fact that the non-CPS world operates with consistency and advance planning. Predictable room assignments and student rosters are standard. Partners were not running charities: The school needed to respect minimum enrollment requirements, scholarship caps, and payment schedules. If a partner disappointed a client because of the school's incompetence, it would be the partner's reputation that would suffer. The success or failure of the community school would hinge on the resource coordinator's ability to steward the program.

Fourth, *not every partner would turn out to be the best fit*. For example, in the very first winter schedule, Jane's Place offered a parent-supervised, cooperative playgroup for very young children. The partnership, formed when a fire left a popular neighborhood cooperative searching for a new home, appeared to be mutually beneficial to all stakeholders. The cooperative came with all its own play equipment and supplies, and it only needed two empty classrooms on the ground floor to set up shop. The school hoped that the arrangement would give neighborhood parents an opportunity to become comfortable with the school long before their children were ready for kindergarten.

Unfortunately, reality proved to be significantly different than what had been planned on paper. Unlike other Jane's Place offerings that lasted about an hour, cooperative parents intended to spend the entire morning at the school, come hell or high water. Without Nettelhorst teachers policing the situation, these parents, who had already paid for the day, thought little of letting children work out their momentary tantrums in the hallway rather than trudge them home in the snow. Suddenly, the noise was leading teachers to close all the classroom doors that Susan had worked so hard to keep open. The situation warranted Nettelhorst's dissolution of the partnership after just one week, knowing that a nasty breakup might lead neighborhood parents to again question the school's competence. First and foremost, Nettelhorst—and Jane's Place by extension—needed to be in the business of education.

And finally, the spectacular demise of the cooperative partnership taught the school a fifth lesson: *Partners were signing up to be part of the new Camp Nettelhorst*. The school would inevitably frustrate partners if they only saw themselves as co-opting space to generate revenue. If a partner couldn't appreciate that the school, in spite of all the charming eccentricities and foibles endemic to public education, was fighting the good fight, the relationship was in trouble from the start. For example, a partner hated that Nettelhorst basketball games could, on rare occasions, run into overtime, pushing back its own program's start time. Whereas other partners might have happily spent the extra ten minutes cheering the Stallions on to victory, this partner believed the gym was on its own private meter. At the end of the day, it didn't matter that the partner ran a successful or popular program: The fit wasn't right. The marketing team's original tag "Jane's Place: Where all the pieces come together" proved to be sage—at least straight from the box, all the pieces needed to fit or the puzzle would never come together down the line. Ultimately, every partner needed to come out of the gate understanding that Nettelhorst had gone to all this trouble in order to serve its children.

Nettelhorst invited the community in even before the school gained the right to call itself a community school. Reformers relentlessly pursued anyone who might be willing to bring their expertise and enthusiasm to Nettelhorst. They leveraged the school's limited resources and capitalized on market forces to turn relationships into deep, mutually beneficial partnerships. Susan was willing to open Nettelhorst's doors to anyone who offered the greater school community something of value. It was this welcoming spirit that enabled a farmers' market, a series of neighborhood events, and the innovative community school partnerships. Ultimately, reformers could have done somersaults until the end of time to bring prospective parents to Nettelhorst's front door, but it all would have been for naught had the school refused to open it.

# FOUR

# ACADEMICS

## RAISE THE BAR

W HILE THE infrastructure team gussied up the school and the special events and enrichment teams created partnerships and leveraged resources, the curriculum team struggled to answer the reform movement's most pressing question: Would Nettelhorst be viable as an academic institution?

The Co-op's curriculum team consisted of park parents who were former teachers, child psychiatrists, psychologists, and linguists—people who were knowledgeable about student development. First, the curriculum team, led by supermoms Lisa Vahey, Karen Gould, and Jennifer Clark, sized up the competition by visiting Chicago's best-regarded public, private, and parochial schools. Once the team had a sense of the caliber of the other schools, it focused on Nettelhorst's curriculum, teachers, discipline protocols, and test scores. Susan allowed the team to inspect Nettelhorst's annual budget, professional development plans, and School Improvement Planning for Advancing Academic Achievement (SIPAAA)—the biannual planning tool required by state law. She gave the team carte blanche to assess data. She allowed select team members (with professional credentials) to observe teachers in their classrooms. In retrospect, it is hard to imagine a principal more willing to open her school to outsiders, warts and all. Four-and-a-half months into its intense research, the team reported that Nettelhorst had a ways to go academically, but it was on the right track.

## WORKING TO CHANGE WHAT CAN BE CHANGED; ACCEPTING WHAT CANNOT

Originally, co-op parents thought they would need to write a new curriculum for the school. As it turns out, the State of Illinois has curriculum pretty much locked up; all schools must cover the same subject matter, and the state holds all schools to the same educational standard. The curriculum team did find, however, that it could markedly influence the way in which the school taught that standards-based curriculum. The team knew that class size would be a deal breaker for most neighborhood families when private schools could boast as few as fourteen students to one teacher. If, however, the board refused to pay for added enrichment positions because the school's enrollment dipped too low, it was fiscally irresponsible for the school to draw on discretionary funds to pay for them out of pocket. As painful as the exercise would be, the school needed to redline extra positions from the annual budget until enrollment improved and the board would foot the bill.

Naturally, the curriculum team would have loved to see a full-time art teacher, a full-time librarian, or even an assistant principal, but the school needed to ensure small class sizes to attract neighborhood parents; if neighborhood enrollment did not increase, the board would respond by cutting teachers or even closing the school outright. Even as the board closed underperforming and underutilized schools throughout Chicago and had publicly threatened to close another elementary school located just blocks away, Nettelhorst's teachers remained oblivious to the school's fate. Susan delivered the bitter pill without dragging the curriculum team into the fray, and crossed her fingers that the neighborhood would show up in force.

Beyond budgetary issues, Susan allowed the curriculum team to help shape Nettelhorst's academic focus. When the board phased out the International Scholars magnet designation across the system, the team encouraged Nettelhorst to choose a Fine and Performing Arts Magnet Cluster School designation instead, but retain the old "International" heading. Thus Nettelhorst became the system's only International Fine and Performing Arts Magnet Cluster School. Because of the standards-based curriculum, Nettelhorst would still teach reading, math, and science, but even if state funding shrunk, art, music, and drama would remain in the school.

As teaching and staff positions opened, Susan allowed co-op parents to play an active role in the hiring process. In an unorthodox move, she encouraged parents to help evaluate résumés, sit in on interviews, ask questions of candidates, and offer their recommendations. By opening the process, parents could see for themselves that Nettelhorst received roughly a thousand applicants for every position, many of whom were stellar. The talent pool was impressive: Most CPS candidates, particularly Teach for America candidates, held advanced degrees from elite institutions and offered impressive employment histories. Whereas reformers imagined that a public elementary school would be struggling to find competent teachers, they soon discovered that each time a teaching position became available, scores of highly qualified individuals would be in the running. Because the competition was so fierce, Nettelhorst could even fill TBP aide positions with experienced teachers who held advanced degrees and subspecialty endorsements.

Because the candidates were all first-rate teachers, Susan didn't see much harm in allowing the core reformers to weigh in on hiring decisions. If parents could not be present at the formal interview, Susan was able to obtain their thoughts later as the candidates would typically pop outside to the playground to meet any neighborhood parents who happened to be around at the time. While few of the reformers outside the curriculum team had any formal training in early childhood education, they could certainly gauge which candidates seemed creative, enthusiastic, or approachable. If a teacher proved to be disappointing, reformers couldn't blame the principal for poor judgment. Reformers, too, had met with the teacher, asked questions, reviewed the same curriculum vitae, and formed the same conclusion. Neighborhood parents would need to accept the reality that new hires don't always perform as expected.

The curriculum team's endorsement went a long way toward mollifying skeptical neighborhood parents who feared that Nettelhorst would not be challenging enough for their precious children, all of whom seemed to be "gifted." The team insisted that the school's low scores were a nonissue; scores would improve just as soon as neighborhood families invested in Nettelhorst with their own children, stabilizing the population and assuredly providing more in school parental support to the current students. While the upper-grade scores hovered in the 50 percent range, these students were performing remarkably well given the myriad challenges that often accompany poverty, against which most of the upper-grade students struggled. When the neighborhood TBP students reached third grade, they would take the ISAT test for the first time, at which point the team suspected that the school's test scores would be comparable to those from Chicago's well-established, selective enrollment magnet schools.[1] When the trusted curriculum team concluded that Nettelhorst was positioned to deliver a quality education in a matter of months, not years, the leap of faith seemed far less daunting.

Susan did, however, overrule two of the curriculum team's key recommendations. In spite of the exodus of some less abled teachers in Susan's first two years, the curriculum team argued that Nettelhorst should follow the lead of some affluent school districts by setting up a Web-based classroom video surveillance system. If anxious parents could check in on their children throughout the day, surely Susan's leap of faith wouldn't seem so risky.

Susan immediately rejected the parent voyeurism solution on the basis that she had already established an open-door policy that would allow parents to volunteer in their child's classroom. She welcomed parents' involvement in the school; peering in from a distant portal would not achieve that goal, nor would it really give parents a complete picture of their child's daily experiences. Additionally, teachers were already bristling under the increased parental scrutiny; the arrival of Big Brother would surely push them over the edge. At some point, nervous parents would need to muster the faith to believe that Nettelhorst's teachers were doing their job.

The team also suggested that Nettelhorst should follow the lead of successful neighborhood schools that lured middle-class families by creating school-within-a-school gifted programs that essentially included *any* student who graduated from the school's TBP program. Susan believed that separating the "Red Jays" from the "Blue Birds" was pedagogically unsound and morally bankrupt; all children were capable of learning. She insisted that "differentiated instruction," the practice of grouping and regrouping students by ability, already worked well at Nettelhorst, and would only improve with increased teacher collaboration and supervision. Again, she welcomed parents' assistance in the classroom. If a student needed additional, individualized attention, more hands on deck could help teachers maintain a more rigorous academic pace for the rest of the class.

While reformers relished the ability to "mind the store," they feared that Nettelhorst wouldn't be able to attract neighborhood families without a conventional tracking system or a separate gifted program. Susan asked parents to stop seeing gifted or tracking programs as some kind of educational Holy Grail and imagine the curriculum in broader terms. If prospective parents toured Nettelhorst and concluded, "I like how the adults treat the children. I like the way the building feels. I like how the children are engaged in their activities," all these intangibles were intimately connected to the idea of curriculum, even for high-performing children.

Susan asked parents to imagine that everything in a child's life, from the second he leaves home until the moment he returns, could be profoundly important. Even "gifted" children learned while waiting in line, eating lunch, playing outside, or even going to the bathroom. If children walked to school holding their parent's hand and stopped to examine something as beautiful as a new crocus or as routine as a meter maid doling out parking tickets, it all mattered. Every time a caring adult took the time to explain anything to a child, no matter how simple, it registered. It was this kind of sensitivity that Susan hoped to instill in all of her teachers.

## ADDRESSING THE NEEDS OF A
## DIVERSE STUDENT POPULATION

Even if Nettelhorst's teaching staff adopted Susan's "whole child" philosophy, it would still need to account for Nettelhorst's current population and its potential student population. In 2001, the board decided
to allow Nettelhorst to cease busing in students from other neighborhood's overcrowded schools, gambling that the school's dynamics
would improve further if students and parents made a conscious choice
to attend Nettelhorst. A large percentage of parents of the bused-in
population recognized the school's potential and elected to keep their
children enrolled, even though this decision meant that they needed
to arrange alternate transportation for their children's travel to and
from Nettelhorst. For some children, this meant taking public transportation each way, sometimes with multiple transfers. As soon as Nettelhorst stopped mandatory busing and required families to make a
conscious choice to stay, the school's climate rapidly improved.

While most community members applauded the end of busing in
students from overcrowded schools, the fact remained that incoming
neighborhood children would not displace any current students. Regardless of however many middle-class neighborhood children opted to enroll,
in all certainty, Nettelhorst's student body would include a large disadvantaged population for several years. Moreover, as a neighborhood
school, CPS required Nettelhorst to accept any child who lived within
the school's attendance boundary regardless of aptitude. And while real
estate values had been climbing steadily since the seventies, the composi-
tion of housing was a blend of multimillion-dollar homes, co-ops, condominiums, rental properties, single-room occupancy, and subsidized
housing. If Nettelhorst could attract local children, it could expect a mixture of affluent families as well as those of more modest economic means.

While most park parents claimed that economic diversity was one of
the great advantages of public school, the curriculum team worried that
prospective middle-class parents would be spooked by Nettelhorst's siz-

able low-income population. Susan wasn't taken aback by such politically incorrect sentiments, conceding that some of the team's concerns were indeed legitimate: Low-income students do face many challenges at home that can impede the process of teaching and learning. And, yes, more advantaged neighborhood families would shoulder some responsibility to help level the playing field. But—so long as everyone was being brutally honest—disadvantaged students often exhibited the same negative behaviors as their advantaged friends, namely laziness, selfishness, and arrogance. All children, regardless of economic background, were capable of similar behavioral patterns and were able to learn.

The curriculum team also voiced the un-PC concern that Nettelhorst's sizable special education population would be off-putting to prospective neighborhood parents. Some prospective parents feared that autistic children whose IEP placed them in regular education classes for some of the school day, would inevitably compromise classroom dynamics, a sentiment rarely voiced in public. If a student's IEP did warrant individualized attention, the board provided a one-on-one teacher aide. While everyone wanted lower teacher/student ratios, most prospective parents believed that inclusion was, at the very least, a mixed blessing.

Everyone had heard the park rumors of public school inclusion classrooms run amok: classroom parents forced to sit idly by when a special needs student hijacked a teacher's attention or physically or verbally assaulted other children. If an experiment in inclusion derailed, park parents would have little if any tolerance for a lumbering bureaucracy to self-correct. Even if the experiment worked in practice, how would Nettelhorst pay for extra classroom aides or escorts when it didn't have enough money to buy pencils and paper? Although most park parents espoused sensitivity, many were secretly fearful that inclusion would negatively impact their own children.

Susan patiently explained that part of the answer was rooted in Illinois law: Public schools were required to provide equal services; therefore, the board, when prodded, provided the extra resources to do so. Children were not the ones who needed to be educated. Although she would explain state mandates, for some prospective parents this news was a bitter pill to swallow.

Susan believed that the presence of special education children in the building was an *opportunity* that benefitted everyone. Twenty years of early childhood experience had taught her that good teachers would provide for *all* students—the ones that can focus, the ones that need to be drawn out, and the ones that can barely contain themselves. Moreover, nothing would change as children moved up through the grades; each student would remain unique. In good classrooms, these disparities among the students are emphasized and embraced rather than compromised by teaching to the 'middle' of the group. Through inclusion, Nettelhorst could offer neighborhood children a robust education and essential character building, as well.

Once the neighborhood parents saw her inclusion theories in practice, Susan insisted that they would come to believe that integrated classrooms were not just tolerable, but *better*. When inclusive classrooms were properly supervised, the students could learn to help their peers and teachers could collaborate more effectively. Plus, the parents were always welcome to volunteer in the classroom to help smooth any rough edges or fill in any gaps. While the curriculum team was skeptical that Nettelhorst would be able to offer a quality education to the neighborhood's most academically advanced students, Susan wasn't even remotely worried that her school could meet everyone's needs, regardless of background or ability.

## IMPROVING A DYSFUNCTIONAL TEACHING CLIMATE

While the jury may have been out on differentiated instruction, both Susan and the curriculum team agreed that Nettelhorst's teaching climate presented a serious challenge. Susan's early initiatives to develop social relationships with and among the teachers were not entirely successful. In spite of many social occasions, holiday celebrations, and tokens of appreciation, many teachers chose to remain isolated. Without the genuine collaboration that Susan was trying to inspire, it was questionable just how much the school's academics would actually improve.

The curriculum team wasn't having much luck bringing the teachers together, either. On the first day of school, the team delivered baskets of peaches donated by the Nettelhorst French Market farmers to each staff member with cute, handwritten notes saying how much they appreciated their efforts. Yet to the parents' dismay, teachers offered few acknowledgments, and in one case, a basket of peaches was discovered untouched in a waste bin. In another instance, when one of the most prestigious hair salons in Chicago opened a new store across the street from the school, the Co-op arranged a free session that included the works—haircuts, color, highlights—for every teacher in the school. Again, there were few acknowledgments, either to co-op parents or the salon. When Susan went to the store to thank the manager personally, the manager reported that some teachers didn't even bother to keep their appointments, some gave them away to others, and some didn't show their appreciation for the service by tipping. Clearly, the problems with the teaching staff ran much deeper than the reformers had realized.

While it might not matter if teachers enjoyed their colleagues or their principal, it was vital that they did a good job teaching. Many of Nettelhorst's teachers performed well, and some performed at an exceptional competency level; however, the construct of the environment insulated their abilities within their four classroom walls. What Susan envisioned, and what the curriculum team was banking on, was that the good and superior teachers would improve exponentially if they were able to escape their silo experiences and create a dynamic network of educators—learning from, building upon, and mapping across each other's successful teaching strategies and innovative ideas. While the curriculum team suspected that parental pressures would help raise the academic bar, and engender cross-classroom collaboration, it doubted whether change would come as swiftly or dramatically as Susan hoped or imagined. However, her faith that her teachers would become great just as soon as their classroom communities demanded greatness was a lot to swallow. Luckily, the end results proved she was right all along—teaching styles changed based on children's academic needs, and blossomed with the shift in how all the players interacted on this educational stage.

## UNSATISFACTORY TEACHERS

Although most of the teachers worked at a functional performance level and some even worked at an exceptional competency level, several less abled teachers remained, and it was doubtful that they had any interest in changing their ways. During the first year of the movement, the curriculum team hoped that prospective parents would not discover all the skeletons in the closet. Co-op tour leaders led prospective parents on serpentine paths through the building to avoid encounters with the few remaining problematic teachers. If parents did observe some questionable behavior on the tour, Susan didn't flinch. She would say that the parents were describing a situation that sounded intolerable; however, because she didn't personally see it, her hands were tied. It was a question of evidence. Unless parents stepped up to the plate to document poor teaching, under the union's competency guidelines, substandard teachers would likely remain in their positions indefinitely.

To prospective parents who had no personal experience with the complex politics of public school, recalcitrant, unionized teachers spelled trouble. A full-page *New York Times* advertisement captures just how fed up parents had become with substandard teachers: A private entity implored readers to help rid public schools of "bad apples" by voting for "the worst unionized teachers in America" and offered a cash reward if the winners stopped teaching forever.[2] When asked, Susan explained just how incredibly difficult it was for public school principals to fire unmotivated, poorly performing teachers.

Predictably, prospective parents viewed poor teaching as a deal breaker; after all, wasn't teaching the school's most important job? Susan argued that Nettelhorst's current teachers were more or less typical of most CPS schools: Some were good, some were great, and some were just okay. To some extent, reformers were just going to need to trust that the principal had their backs. The curriculum team, however, was hardly sanguine. Even if Nettelhorst shuffled underperforming instructors into upper-grade classrooms, eventually the reformers' luck would run out, and their children would be subjected to subpar teaching at some point. Susan asserted that any school, public or private, would always have a few teachers who weren't top-notch instructors. There would be some teachers parents liked and some that they didn't; there would be some teachers who would have a weak rapport with parents but a natural affinity for children, and vice versa. She maintained that while not every teaching style would be the ideal fit for every child, children would learn valuable lessons. While some reformers remained concerned that the school board and the teachers union seemed to tolerate incompetence, most were satisfied that Nettelhorst's teaching staff would continue to improve and that the students would benefit.

Some members of the curriculum team were dubious that the lowest-performing teachers would ever be up to snuff, but Susan asserted that teaching was, to some extent, inconsequential. At first blush, this seemed to be a curious position for a lifetime educator. What she meant was that children, when supported at home, learn invaluable skills in any environment. School was about teaching skills for life, and part of life was learning to deal with difficult situations. Susan argued that parents were not doing their kids any favors by removing every difficulty in their path. Even while Nettelhorst continued to weed out the few less abled teachers and children sometimes experienced a distracting classmate, students would learn valuable coping skills. Children who encountered a moderate degree of adversity would learn to marshal the inner resources necessary to deal with the ordinary frustrations of daily life. "Someday, your little babies will grow up and deal with someone who is difficult," she reasoned, "like a boss, a professor, a coworker, or even a first husband or wife." At that point, their grown children would dig deep and draw on all the fine lessons they learned at Nettelhorst.

While her "children learn from adversity" argument might satisfy some of the most risk-tolerant parents, the curriculum team wasn't buying it. Most park parents weren't the much-ridiculed, "snowplow" types, desperately trying to clear away any potential difficulty from their child's path. A year spent enduring a bad teacher might very well encourage resilience and coping skills, but at what cost? It was one thing to ask children to adapt to a range of teaching styles, but quite another to defeat the primary purpose of sending them to school altogether.

While the process of firing a tenured teacher was difficult and time-consuming, Nettelhorst needed to persevere. The team fully understood that the process, with its detailed procedures and exact timelines, was not for the fainthearted: A principal must create documentation through a detailed case report, visit the teacher's classroom multiple times, assign an independent mentor to the teacher, observe the mentor observing the teacher, and then write a response to the observation. Although the board offers to help principals navigate the complex discipline and dismissal procedures, Chicago's teachers' union, understandably, goes to considerable lengths to protect its members.

If the case does go to arbitration, the onus is on the principal to prove that the teacher is unsatisfactory, a charge that carries a high burden of proof. If the principal makes any mistake in the paperwork or filing, or if the teacher takes a leave of absence, complies with any discipline recommendations, or appears to be improving during remediation in any way, the case is dismissed. The principal must then wait a certain period of time, and if she has the stamina, can begin the arduous process all over again. All these efforts, of course, are to be carried out above and beyond the normal day's work for the principal.

Susan knew the pitfalls of this process all too well: During her first year at Nettelhorst, she dismissed an underperforming teacher, only to find herself served with a federal whistle-blower lawsuit. Aside from the personal toll it exacted, the lawsuit meant that the board was taking a wait-and-see approach to her leadership, much in the same way that Nettelhorst's teachers were hedging their bets to see if she would last in the job. Because she knew she wasn't guilty of any wrongdoing, she tried to stay out of the board's way as best she could and to focus her energy on removing teachers who were not performing to minimum standards, giving the rest the opportunities they needed to become more successful.

Susan and the curriculum team agreed that Nettelhorst's teaching standards were all over the map. While most teachers were adequate and some were stellar, some had no business being in *any* public school classroom. Some teachers would swear at students and adults. One teacher muttered nonsensical gibberish and obscenities as she walked down the hall. Another had a restraining order issued against her for hitting students. Even though these instructors rarely collaborated with other teachers and left school at three o'clock sharp daily, they still impeded the learning environment well beyond their own classrooms; their negativity fermented dissent, even among Nettelhorst's most capable teachers, and created a climate of hostility and unrest. Until Susan's lawsuit was dismissed, the board was wary of intervening on her behalf as she tried to manage these few challenging teachers and the distressing situations they unfortunately prompted.

Some might find it unseemly for a principal to empower "vigilante" parents to help document unacceptable behavior when they encountered it. But when an underserved classroom has little to no parental involvement and the principal cannot be in all places at once to monitor the faculty, this becomes the only realistic option. It is certain that the teachers in question believed themselves to be competent, and perhaps they once had been. Unfortunately, this was no longer the case. While no one encouraged or condoned harassment, which would have laid the groundwork for yet another nasty lawsuit, parents were able to confront "unsatisfactory" teaching head-on from behind the scenes.

In an unexpected twist, when Susan finally managed to rid Nettelhorst of most of the less abled teachers, the remaining staff members, including some very competent ones, misinterpreted their colleagues' departures and viewed them as martyrs. Many teachers who even voiced agreement with Susan's assessment protested the final outcome all the same. It is unclear whether their protest was motivated by solidarity or self-preservation, but the fact that these expelled teachers still held sway long after they were gone showed just how much power they had wielded within the building.

While conventional wisdom suggests that all members of the school community need to buy into reform, Nettelhorst's negative teaching faction was so influential that the Roscoe Park Eight shied away from including teachers until the building could stabilize. Initially, most teachers didn't know what to think of these meddlesome neighborhood parents but were hesitant to get involved, assuming that they, too, would soon be whisked away. To illustrate, when the Co-op invited teachers to submit "wish lists" for their classrooms, only *one* teacher responded that her classroom needed *a single* item, a tape recorder. Perhaps the teachers doubted that anything would ever come of the request. Or, even if they thought that the Co-op could have delivered, most teachers were taking cues from their disgruntled colleagues. Strangers had suddenly appeared in their classrooms with clipboards, so teachers were reluctant to embrace any initiative that appeared to come by way of a Trojan horse.

Moreover, few teachers volunteered to help community volunteers improve the school's infrastructure during the first year of the movement. When Chicago Cares, a not-for-profit organization that mobilizes community volunteers and resources to help renovate the city's parks and public schools, brought its annual Serve-a-Thon to Nettelhorst, only *one* teacher joined the hundreds of volunteers who came to paint the school. As reformers and pro bono artists and contractors painted after school and on weekends, only two teachers ever volunteered their time. Even when artists invited students to help paint murals during the school day, teachers refused to work alongside them. As volunteers painted, cleaned, or carried furniture, some teachers would ignore them or simply offer a polite "hello." Some went as far as to curse them under their breath. With few exceptions, the teachers made it painfully clear that the new parents might be tolerated, but they certainly weren't welcome.

The exceptions were notable. A handful of sympathetic and encouraging staff members deserve much credit for buoying the early reformers' spirits, and clearing obstacles in their path. Most of the Co-op's early supporters had been at Nettelhorst for decades and filled key positions in the school: the school counselor, the administrative assistant; the building engineer; the janitors, and some veteran teachers, primarily in the lower grades. Every positive action, whether known or unknown, bidden or unbidden, helped to propel the reform movement forward.

But this support, however genuine, rarely surfaced in public. When Susan invited Jacqueline and Nicole to address the teachers, the meeting confirmed the suspicion that they felt the neighborhood parents were up to no good. In advance of an all-school assembly to trumpet the new community school, Susan decided to introduce the co-op's cofounders using a one-two punch at a mandatory professional development day: First, an outside educational expert would encourage the teachers to be less myopic, and then the two women would come in to explain how the new community school would benefit the entire school community.

The Co-op's much-anticipated debut turned into a date with the firing squad. Jacqueline and Nicole walked into the teachers' lounge, a room that the infrastructure team had renovated just months before, completely unaware of what had just transpired in the meeting. They surveyed their virtually all-female, seemingly self-segregated audience: The African American teachers glared at them from one side of the room, the Hispanic teachers glowered from the other, and the white teachers sat in the middle of the room, staring down at the floor. The teachers' questions were pointed and hostile, but valid. Why were the neighborhood parents taking the school away from them? Who had sent them? What would a community school really offer Nettelhorst students? How did neighborhood parents expect to get away with this land grab?

Jacqueline and Nicole tried to hold their ground as they explained the genesis and purpose of Jane's Place. The only male teacher in the room rallied to their defense: "It sounds like you two have put a great deal of work into this community school grant," the teacher said. "Clearly, there are details to work out, but it all sounds very promising." As the interminably long hour wound down, Susan thanked the women for coming, turned to her teachers, and said calmly, "Perhaps all of you aren't aware, but these women represent hundreds of people in the community who desperately want Nettelhorst to succeed."

Jacqueline and Nicole left the staff meeting completely stunned. The Co-op had pressed an overly optimistic time frame, but there was no way to slow the machinery down. Too many people were involved, and the school had made too many promises.

As the women walked through the school's freshly painted hallway, Jacqueline turned to her friend and said, "Well, that was a waste of nine months. Who did we think we were kidding?" Nicole, ever positive, replied, "Give the teachers time; they'll come around. Our community school is going to be one of those 'If you build it, they will come' kind of deals." Susan shot her head out of the teachers' lounge, calling for them to stop; she mouthed the word "sorry" and then returned to her teachers to control the damage.

The Roscoe Park Eight knew full well that Susan was an administrator and could ill afford to alienate her staff. Yet the teachers' open hostility begs the question: Why did some teachers seemingly despise the park parents when they knew so little about them? One possible explanation is that some teachers may have resented the fact that outsiders who didn't have children in the school were suddenly intruding on their turf and interfering with the business of teaching. Some teachers begrudged the fact that these civilians, who obviously knew so little about early childhood education, suddenly had their principal's ear. Another possible explanation is that some teachers feared that the neighborhood parents intended to repeat the tired story of gentrification—privileged white parents with scant interest in educating underprivileged black and Latino children from overcrowded schools would force them out. Clearly, there were unspoken concerns that despite the public school "we honor diversity" mantra, it wouldn't be long before the "undesirable elements" were ousted to make room for privileged white children.

While these sentiments went largely unspoken in public, deep-seated fears and prejudices bubbled just below the surface. For example, some minority teachers alleged that the new bistro mural by the lunchroom represented only Caucasians, proving in their minds that the co-op artists didn't celebrate diversity. The post-impressionistic fresco depicted figures sporting lavender, blue, and green faces, upscale clothing, and their pet poodles dining at a French cafe. To these teachers, the mural was a visual representation of the racist tide that was stealthily gaining force.

The concern that Nettelhorst would become a predominantly white school was not entirely unfounded given Chicago's long history of racial segregation; however, it was unlikely that history would repeat itself in East Lakeview. In spite of the gentrification that began in the seventies, the East Lakeview/Boystown area still maintained considerable diversity. Unless Nettelhorst became a selective enrollment magnet school, its student body would always reflect the immediate neighborhood. Moreover, affirmative action laws would continue to apply to Nettelhorst, just as they did to every other Chicago public school.

In the absence of any parental participation in the upper grades, Susan tried to mitigate socioeconomic threats by demanding that park parents fill the void. Neighborhood parents were expected to host upper-grade holiday parties, reading nights, and pizza parties, and to fill the otherwise empty auditorium for upper-grade assemblies. She insisted that older students needed just as much love and support as those in the younger grades, and that any parental surrogate would fit the bill. She also insisted that the Co-op translate every memo into Spanish, even though the school's Spanish-only population was small. Because many similar movements across the country unraveled when reformers appeared to be insensitive to the diverse voices within their school community, the school tried to err on the side of respect and inclusiveness.

To be fair, most teachers did not see the reformers' agenda as elitist or racist; nonetheless, they remained guardedly aloof, waiting to see how the power struggle in the school would play out. They figured one of several things would happen—the principal would continue to lead her school, the LSC would refuse to extend her four-year contract, or the lawsuit filed in federal court would force her resignation. As the negative faction had run every other administrator out of town, the smart money said that the principal was sitting on packed suitcases, and when forced out, she would take her new, meddlesome friends with her.

Because the teachers were not prepared to jump on the reform band-wagon en masse, the Co-op chose to fly low on the radar until the principal could wrest control. To be clear, the Co-op valued the teachers and would have loved their support, but they had already rebuffed the Co-op's initial gestures. Given Nettelhorst's less-than-amiable climate, any grand overture to the teachers was risky. If the negative teaching faction had something or someone concrete to rally against, it could easily have pointed its guns at the park parents. Given the pummeling Jacqueline and Nicole endured at the first teacher meet-and-greet, how well would the other park parents fare? If race or class issues erupted in force, the Co-op's public relations team would be hard-pressed to control the backlash in the media. If the reform movement became a political liability, local politicians and school board officials would likely take a giant step back.

## CONTENDING WITH A DYSFUNCTIONAL LOCAL SCHOOL COUNCIL

In addition to Nettelhorst's disgruntled teachers, a small but vocal faction of parent and community representatives hamstrung the LSC, the group charged with stewarding the school's academic health. These LSC members believed Nettelhorst had failed them (or their children) in some overt way—and perhaps it had. At first, the curriculum team tried to win over these discontented parents with pledges to resolve key issues, but it became clear immediately that nothing short of the principal's dismissal would appease them. The group bred dissent by actively stonewalling council meetings, disrupting classes, distributing accusatory flyers in the neighborhood, petitioning the board, and even taking the extreme step of suing other members of the council.

Of course, Nettelhorst's students suffered the most from an LSC that claimed to be acting in their interests while behaving otherwise. For example, some members of the LSC accused the administration of mismanaging library funds and ordered an internal audit; consequently, children could not take books out for over six months. In 1995, the state of Illinois created local school councils (LSCs) comprised of locally elected parent, teacher, and community representatives, in addition to the principal—in order to give communities more local control of the schools in their neighborhoods. Each LSC would determine and oversee their school's budget (SIPPA), and also had the power to hire and fire their own principal. In practice, however, LSCs could become so polarized and acrimonious that regular school business suffered. By the time the Roscoe Park Eight arrived on the scene, Nettelhorst's dysfunctional LSC had so effectively hobbled the administration that the school library couldn't even loan books!

Until the LSC became a functional, positive entity for the school, park parents tried to stay clear of the fray. It was painful to watch. At one LSC meeting, the leader of the school's volunteer tutors stood up to deliver his monthly progress report to the council. When a two-minute timer rang out, the chair cut him off mid-sentence and ordered him to sit down at once, contending that "the council had heard quite enough." The eighty-year-old volunteer leader, who had tutored Nettelhorst's struggling readers every week for years, slumped to his seat in dismay. At the same meeting, Jacqueline, who had come only to explain the impending community school grant to the council and gain its official approval, rose to her feet and blurted, "This is insane! You have one chance to pull yourself out of the mess you are in. If you can't pull together, this opportunity is going to pass you by, and it will never come again. No one can help you if guys can't stop this nonsense. Right *now!*" And with that, she stormed out of the library. Because the reformers were trying to fly under the radar, Nicole represented the Co-op at LSC meetings from then on.

## THE EXODUS OF THE SCHOOL'S NEGATIVE FACTION

Much to everyone's amazement, these small but vocal groups of disgruntled teachers and LSC members concluded that life would be easier elsewhere; they packed up and left Nettelhorst, *voluntarily*, in one fell swoop. Why did individuals who had wielded so much power for decades give up so quickly? In the case of the LSC, when the board decided to stand behind the LSC vote to renew the principal's four-year contract, the negative parent representatives sensed that the game was over. One parent transferred her child to another school, and the child of one of the other parent representatives graduated. The two community representatives (a mother-daughter team) lost interest when the federal court ultimately vindicated Susan completely. On the teacher front, Susan and the curriculum team worked together to intensify existing university partnerships and forge new ones, enabling many educational experts to observe teachers, conduct interviews, and document teaching styles. Predictably, not everyone felt comfortable working in such an open, collaborative environment, and several teachers opted to retire or find more suitable accommodation elsewhere.

Whatever their rationale for leaving, their departure immediately triggered improvements in the professional environment. Susan was able to quickly fill the newly opened positions with high-caliber candidates, many from Teach for America. These energetic, young leaders infused the school with new ideas and possibilities. Their infectious enthusiasm helped to draw out Nettelhorst's seasoned professionals and, as a group, this powerhouse of talent embarked on its journey toward a solitary goal—providing stellar academic opportunities for Nettelhorst's students.

Today, Nettelhorst's teaching team has impressive credentials, complete with myriad teaching awards, professional development grants, national certifications, and university partnerships. The teaching climate engenders innovative thinking and collaboration that is apparent to students and parents alike. Without exception, Nettelhorst teachers all share a common vision that always puts children first, but this happy state of affairs did not fall from the sky; it grew from the ground up.

# FIVE

# SELL THE DREAM

## REBRAND AND REPOSITION

N O ONE WAS going to hear about the new community school, the fantastic curriculum, or the beautifully decorated interior if the Co-op's marketing team couldn't entice potential parents to visit. As it stood, most park parents were deeply skeptical of CPS in general—and skeptical of Nettelhorst, in particular, if they had heard the park rumors. How could the marketing team convince a skittish neighborhood that a "new and improved" Nettelhorst was worth a second look?

### EXTERNAL MARKETING

Before the Roscoe Park Eight arrived at Nettelhorst, the school's entire marketing plan hinged on the success of the TBP program to hook neighborhood families. However, the school struggled to maintain the minimum enrollment of just eighteen children. CPS offered to help solve Nettelhorst's TBP enrollment problem by threatening to close the school's TBP program down, permanently. Although the school was desperate for neighborhood families to enroll preschool children, the entirety of its rags-to-riches recruitment scheme consisted of a large yellow-and-blue, vinyl banner hung on the playground fence that read

"Nettelhorst Tuition-based Preschool, call 773.534.5810 for information." Sadly, if a prospective parent called the school, it was doubtful that anyone would pick up the phone, or if they did, that they would have any information about the program. If parents did come to visit (assuming they could find the front door *and* get it open), the school could only offer them a one-page photocopied sheet on the TBP program, which included clip-art cartoon children, misspellings, and grammatical mistakes. Nettelhorst's future TBP marketing plans at the time included placing an advertisement in one of the local papers and hosting a neighborhood rummage sale.

Susan recognized that the TBP was the key to luring neighborhood families, and she was the first one to admit that the school needed help. Merely hanging a shingle outside was not going to bring in bodies. Few neighborhood families had any idea what the TBP program was, let alone that Nettelhorst had one of the city's first. As it was highly unlikely that anyone was going to visit Nettelhorst, the marketing team suggested that Susan take the TBP children on a field trip to Roscoe Park. She embraced the idea and marched the preschool over to hear a free concert by a popular children's singer. The students had made little fans fashioned from paper plates that read "I ♡ Nettelhorst!" By all accounts, the trip was a success, as most park parents discovered that, to their surprise, real, live, happy children attended Nettelhorst.

Just as importantly, the parents discovered that the school's principal not only welcomed their children but their insight. "Whatever rumors you have heard in the past," she announced over the microphone, "you need to know that Nettelhorst has every potential to become a great school if we all join together to make it happen." For most park parents, the very idea that a public school principal would actively welcome the input of neighborhood parents was unthinkable and intoxicating. The park buzzed for weeks.

The marketing team quickly discovered that most parents learned about public and private schools at the two Northside Parents Network (NPN) school fairs held each fall.[1] Jacqueline and Nicole set off to their first NPN fair to represent the Nettelhorst Parents' Co-op with nothing

Thanks to artist Julia Goldman, Nettelhorst's youngest students pretend to "swim" to lunch via a formerly dark subterranean passageway that became a vibrant underwater mural called Atlantis.

PHOTO: ANGIE GARBOT

On the way to lunch, students make interest-bearing deposits at an in-school, deposit only bank facilitated by Harris Bank and parent volunteers. Mural inspired by author/illustrator Maira Kalman's *Ooh-la-la (Max in Love)*.

PHOTO: ANGIE GARBOT

In honor of the school's namesake, Louis Nettelhorst, the lunchroom became Bistro Louis, thanks to artist Jonna Mulqueen of the Enchanted Room.
PHOTO: ANGIE GARBOT.

Thanks to artist Amy Lemaire, upper grade students have homeroom in the Moroccan world music café. Furnished with donated Crate and Barrel Congo tables and Meadowcraft cushions, the café is a comfortable place for kids to watch movies, play chess and read.
PHOTO: ANGIE GARBOT

Andrew Skwish painted the exterior doors leading to the school's auditorium.

PHOTO: ANGIE GARBOT

Exterior doors painted by artist and Nettelhorst mom Shari Imbo entitled "Lakeview Rhapsody."

PHOTO: ANGIE GARBOT

When Flashy Trash, a beloved neighborhood vintage store, closed its doors, owner Harold Mandel donated a mural by Anita Prentice (now customized).
PHOTO: ANGIE GARBOT

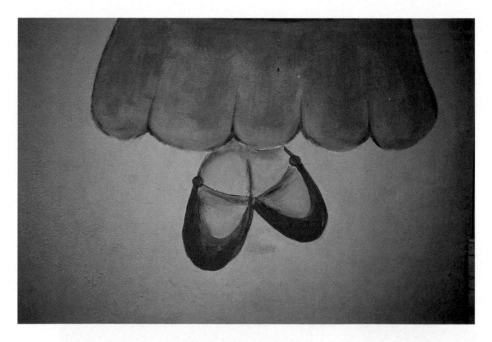

Detail from exterior doors painted by Debbie Egizio.
PHOTO: RON REASON

but colorful postcards advertising the school's January open house. If the marketing team had done its research, though, it would have warned them that each school would have a six-foot table to display its wares: pictures of happy, engaged students; scrapbooks of press clippings; sample lesson plans; balloons with the school's logo; personalized tablecloths and pens; glossy brochures; colorful posters; and even computer videos of the school's highlights. No amount of paraphernalia, however, could have prepared Jacqueline and Nicole for the crush of hundreds and hundreds of overwhelmed, glassy-eyed parents, each more desperate than the one before.

With absolutely nothing to show but their little open house postcards, Jacqueline and Nicole made the best of their situation, standing in front of their empty folding table and shilling their little school like P.T. Barnum.

> "Have you heard what we're doing at Nettelhorst? We're fixing it! That's right! Check us out! It's a great public school with guaranteed admission, so you can forget all this CPS/private school enrollment business right now! And, it's free! That's right, you'll be free and in the clear right through eighth grade! Check us out! We have school partners who are the best of the best. Old Town School of Folk Music! Fairytale Ballet! H.M.D. Academy of Tae Kwon Do! Check us out! Check us out! Check us out!"

No one at the fair had ever heard of Nettelhorst, but it was clear that in a room full of glitz and hype, parents were ready for this refreshingly honest, if overly enthusiastic, pitch by two moms who believed passionately in what they were helping to build for their own children.

## REBRAND AND REPOSITION

After the NPN fair, the marketing team realized that Nettelhorst would need a far more serious recruitment campaign if it wanted to be competitive with the more established schools; "Nettelhorst: not as bad as it used to be, look again!" would not work. Nettelhorst needed to be completely repackaged and resold. The marketing team elected to begin with the preposterous position that Nettelhorst was as good as any elite private or established public magnet school. As long as the team was building castles in the air, better to fabricate a stellar school than a mediocre one.

What angle should the marketing team highlight? The public/private school debate seemed to boil down to cost, so maybe the fact that Nettelhorst offered a free education would appeal to its target audience. After all, parents could save upwards of $200,000 if they chose a public elementary school over a private one. The team suspected that parents who expected to send their children to private school might be willing to settle for a slightly less rigorous educational experience in public school if the decision to do so would not incur any social stigma. However, if the marketing team trumpeted the bargain angle, prospective parents might come to associate Nettelhorst with "the school for cheapskates," which would be less than helpful in articulating the finer points of the institution. The savings advantage could come into play only *after* the school won the quality argument.

But how could the marketing team make an argument for quality when Nettelhorst seemed, in those early days, to have so little going for it? Perhaps Nettelhorst might gain legitimacy by association if the marketing team could trumpet the school's new cultural partnerships and piggyback on their well-deserved reputations. While the park parents might ultimately reject Nettelhorst for their own children, the new "sizzle package" would at least encourage them to give the school a second look.

If Nettelhorst hoped to manage this sleight of hand, it needed to present a more personalized, as well as a more professional, image to whomever might happen to call or stop by. Many of the needed improvements were relatively simple to put into practice. For example, the office clerk needed to answer the phone by saying, "Hello, *The* Nettelhorst School. May I help you?" It is hard to believe that this obvious aspect of customer service needed to be coached, but it was a world away from what previous administrators had tolerated. Similarly, the guidance counselor who handled preschool applications was given the fancy title of admissions counselor. The team encouraged the school to print notices for the front door on thicker paper with sophisticated fonts. It might seem silly to think these marketing ploys had any relevance to what was transpiring inside a kindergarten classroom, but taken together, these efforts presented a unified front for what the school hoped to become.

What look would appeal to East Lakeview parents? Like the infrastructure team, the marketing team, led by supermom Kathy Tuite, opted to capitalize on the school's most salient academic feature as an International Scholars Magnet Site.[2] In order to compete with the private and parochial schools, Nettelhorst needed to have an impressive takeaway informational package. Pro bono graphic designers helped the team to create a cohesive presentation. Inside the folders, prospective parents could find copious amounts of information on all things Nettelhorst. The copy mimicked the style used by Chicago's top private schools and was printed on quality cream-colored paper stock. Each different area of the school had its own logo: The school's primary logo consisted of two interlocking, antique globes; the Jane's Place logo featured two dancing puzzle pieces, one blue and one green, each with a longitude/latitude overlay. While most of the school's targeted demographic actually shopped at thrift stores or Target, they aspired to hip, high-end boutiques. Consequently, the marketing team modeled the Parents' Co-op logo after the Barney's Co-op logo (itself inspired by Robert Indiana's iconic LOVE sculpture). All this material was carefully packaged in glossy folders that drew from a smart palette of sepia and terracotta hues; the folders had an unusual die-cut closure of two interlocking globes and were sealed with a coordinating compass sticker.

To help counteract the impression that the school was created yesterday, all the styling had an antique and old world feel (not such a philosophical leap, as the elementary school had existed for over a century). If Nettelhorst wanted to compete with the private schools, it had to start presenting itself like one; all the marketing materials needed to exude affluence, sophistication, and professionalism.

The marketing team also developed a creative, forward-thinking advertising campaign. Volunteers blanketed the neighborhood with a series of eye-catching posters. One for the TBP showed a child sleeping peacefully, with the tagline, "Think Global, Nap Local." Another placard for kindergarten depicted a horror-struck woman (mirroring Edward Munch's *The Scream*) with the tagline, "Panicked about School? The choice might be right under your nose." The team also designed a series of glossy postcards from a standard template: theme-appropriate student artwork on one side, and color-coordinated information about an upcoming community event on the other side. Postcards became a natural choice as they looked and felt upscale and were quick to design, inexpensive to produce, and easy to distribute. The postcards proved to be so effective in getting the word out that the school continued to produce them even after a local developer donated an electronic message board for Nettelhorst's exterior.

While local businesses printed almost all of the school's marketing materials pro bono, Susan generously offered to use her discretionary funds when the Co-op ran out of luck securing donated services. Years later, the marketing team learned a neat trick: Realtors would readily shoulder the costs to print postcards (roughly two hundred dollars for five thousand cards) if they could commandeer the card's flip side. This was a win-win situation: Realtors could market services beyond their own mailing lists without incurring additional postage, and the school could get free postcards and added hype. Plus, a shared realtor/school postcard would advance the notion of an exclusive Nettelhorst district.

## CREATE A WEB PRESENCE

As interest in Nettelhorst increased, the school needed its own personalized website, one that followed the established content, layout, and theme of the school's hard-copy marketing folders to relay basic information about the school *before* parents came to visit. The school office was woefully understaffed and overburdened already; no one had the time or energy to field questions from inquisitive prospective parents all day. With an informational school website in place, the office clerk could politely recommend that callers check out the school's website, and then come for the weekly tour or call the Jane's Place resource coordinator.

Additionally, a strong presence on the web would help all the co-op teams accomplish their goals. In the world of cyberspace, the marketing team could easily set Nettelhorst on equal footing with all the other established magnet and private schools. The public relations team could help fuel the buzz by sharing media stories and showcasing school and community events beyond the immediate neighborhood. Merchants were more inclined to donate goods or services if the school's website corroborated the solicitor's heartfelt pitch. The curriculum team could explain the school's educational philosophy and methodology in a way that would resonate with its demanding new clientele. And finally, the enrichment team could use the website to promote Jane's Place programming to the greater school community.[3] As the school continued to evolve, the administration assumed more responsibility for the site's content and maintenance, while parents continued to provide content, photos, and links to other parent-led initiatives.

The marketing team also needed to spread the word about Nettelhorst's website to many of the local and national web-based information services that prospective parents typically search in their first wave of school research. If a school doesn't forward detailed information to these sites, their directories will only list the barest information that can be gleaned from publicly available sources, which might paint an incomplete or unflattering picture. The team provided the web-based information services with robust descriptions and accurate facts and statistics.

The marketing team fastidiously monitored what current or prospective parents were saying about Nettelhorst in web-based chat rooms. If negative chatter started to percolate, reformers immediately brought it to Susan's attention, however disheartening it might have been for her to hear the stream of half-truths, paranoia, and constructive criticism. If, in fact, it turned out that a Nettelhorst teacher's venting was stoking the neighborhood's gossip mill, Susan needed to have a talk about discretion and loyalty. If a Nettelhorst parent was the source, the administration needed to work quickly to diffuse the situation. In either case, a few co-op parents needed to post counter opinions to the cyber-discussion immediately. Had Nettelhorst unwittingly created a chilling effect by posting responses under the Co-op's name or its own, it would have defeated the purpose of monitoring the site in the first place.

As much as the school needed to mitigate negative venting in cyberspace, it needed to encourage positive chatter, as well. Many local and national sites allowed principals and parents to post their own comments. The team forwarded letters from the principal to all the sites welcoming prospective parents and trumpeting Nettelhorst's accomplishments and goals, and it encouraged satisfied Nettelhorst parents to submit reviews. Although the marketing team was not above using smoke and mirrors, it was keenly aware that savvy parents had little tolerance for school officials who masqueraded as parents or single parents who issued multiple reviews under numerous aliases.[4] Thus, the school worked to ensure that its practices and information were above reproach to preserve its credibility. The marketing team hoped that a robust picture of Nettelhorst, both on its own website and on general search sites, would entice prospective parents to leave cyberspace and take the school tour, whereupon the school would hopefully sell itself.

## SCHOOL TOURS

Although the school's first open house was a resounding success, with over three hundred families attending, and over seventy children registering for preschool, the extravaganza strained both the school and the Co-op. Moving forward, a weekly school tour might present a less stressful way for neighborhood parents to test the waters. Whereas the competition offered tours once a month, or even once or twice a year, reformers hoped that the frequency and consistency of a weekly tour would make it easier for prospective parents to check out a school that was not on the top of their list.

How could reformers entice neighborhood parents who were only mildly interested in Nettelhorst to visit the school? Reformers landed on a novel idea: They would invite the bookstore across the street, where gay/lesbian titles shared equal footing with children's literature, to offer a weekly neighborhood story time for neighborhood children in the school's library. Ed Devereux, the owner of the bookstore, Unabridged, had offered an in-store children's story time with limited success, so he jumped at the opportunity to reach neighborhood parents. By moving Unabridged's story time to Nettelhorst, the head of the bookstore's children's department, Robert McDonald, was guaranteed an audience at every reading. The TBP and the state pre-kindergarten would send their students and teachers to the library, where the group could effortlessly absorb any neighborhood kids who might materialize. Unabridged could even do cross-promotion by recommending various children's books throughout the bookstore as "Nettelhorst Story Time Favorites."

Unlike the school's unsuccessful neighborhood cooperative playgroup that had targeted the same age demographic, the bookstore's story time had a radically different impact on the school. The free story time reading, which included neighborhood toddlers with Nettelhorst preschoolers, was only forty minutes long and supervised by parents and Nettelhorst teachers. If visiting toddlers became disruptive, parents had the good sense to whisk them home for a nap before they ruined everyone's experience. Without fail, Robert would appear at Nettelhorst every Tuesday to read, all for free. Far from being a chore, Robert found that his time spent reading his favorite stories to children at Nettelhorst was the highlight of his week.

Following story time, parents were encouraged to bring their children on a relaxed, parent-led school tour, and the school worked hard to keep them engaged. Because the huge facility included at least a dozen flights of stairs, small children often needed prodding to keep up. The tour guide would empower kids to act as group leaders, hunting for visual clues: "Stop and point when you reach the airplane!" "Who will be the first one to find the boat?" "When you find the bathtub, climb in it!" Back in the library after the tour, children could play with the squiggly bead-maze, color pictures, or join an ongoing music lesson while their parents asked questions. Though entertained, children were always in the same room as their parents, who were ultimately responsible for their welfare. If a child became particularly disruptive, the empathetic tour leader would gently suggest that the family return another time (reformers learned their lesson from the ill-fated Nettelhorst cooperative playgroup).

Although small children could be distracting on a tour, the benefits of accommodating them were numerous. Parents who were not paying for a babysitter were less cranky and would stay longer; parents were less anxious when they saw that their children were comfortable; and prospective parents were less apprehensive when they saw that Nettelhorst's teachers even treated children who did not yet attend the school with kindness and respect. Many parents, who had arrived for story time with no idea that a tour was even in the cards, wound up staying after the tour so that their kids could play in the Jane's Place toddler gym. With the ease of story time/tour/open gym, prospective parents with very young children could become comfortable with Nettelhorst long before they hit the frenzied school market in earnest.

However, story time could barely soothe prospective parents who came to Nettelhorst actively shopping for schools. Parents living outside the district were especially nervous because they assumed that they were being scrutinized by the school as much as they were evaluating the school. Parents also considering private schools materialized fastidiously scrubbed and painfully self-aware, if only out of habit. The story time proved to be a great introduction, but the Co-op quickly realized that the school needed to go the extra mile to make everyone feel welcome.

Every aspect of a prospective parent's visit to the school had to be considered from arrival onward. Reformers asked Susan to imagine herself in the shoes of a prospective parent visiting Nettelhorst for the first time. Taking the instruction literally, she began by watching the school's visitors via the security camera as they attempted to navigate the front door. She didn't know whether to laugh or cry at what she saw: mothers—their toddlers at their sides—ringing all the buzzers at the door, first the left, then the right, then left again, looking up at the camera, looking behind them, knocking, pulling on the locked doors, looking at watches, and sometimes surrendering.

How could a first-time visitor possibly know that the unmarked button to the right of the door would signal the office clerk to buzz it open? (Not the unmarked button to the *left* of the door, which would only ring in the preschool classrooms following nap time.) Or, how could a visitor guess that a nearly inaudible click signaled a two-second window to pull the door handle before the door relocked? Or, how could a guest know that if no one answered the buzzer, the clerk had likely stepped away from her desk (perhaps for ten minutes or more), and the guest would need to keep trying or call the office by cell phone? If first impressions were paramount, Nettelhorst needed to make some quick fixes. One simple act alleviated this sea of confusion—the school posted a flier on the front door instructing parents how to ring the security buzzer.[5]

No sooner did first-time visitors overcome the door gauntlet than they faced another hurdle: Where to go? Whereas most schools had a security guard posted just inside the front door, Nettelhorst had funding for only one security guard who roamed the building. Consequently, once the office clerk successfully buzzed in the fuzzy human image on the security monitor, the guest was pretty much on his own. Here again, the solution was simple—include instructions on the door flier explaining where visitors could leave coats and strollers and how to navigate to the library. Whenever possible, the Co-op tried to have a smiling parent volunteer welcome prospective parents, whether inside the front door or at the top of the stairs, and then usher them to the library. Hopefully, the well-greeted visitors would be put so at ease from the start that they might ignore the school's woefully lax security.

After the story time ended in the library, the parent tour leader gathered everyone together to watch a soft-sell promotional video of the school. Because the competition showed soul-stirring professional videos at the beginning of its tours, the marketing team decided Nettelhorst needed one, too. The team convinced a local cable company to produce a two-and-a-half-minute video, pro bono, and labored on the voice-over script and background music for weeks to get just the right language, tone, and inflection. Later, as the school gained credibility, the promotional video became superfluous, but during the early days, it helped to instantly convey the school's vision.

After watching the video, the group dashed off to explore the building, and the co-op tour leader explained Nettelhorst's programs at the appropriate juncture. For example, she explained the preschool program when parents were in the preschool classroom, the community school model when in the Jane's Place wing, the healthy choice pilot program when in the lunchroom, and so forth. Each room provided sufficient visual evidence that prospective parents could answer many questions for themselves.[6] The goal was that, by the end of the tour, parents would be so awestruck by the school's infrastructure and vivacity that Susan's "risk of faith" sermon would appear downright logical.

It became clear that the rehearsed sequence worked better than having Susan greet the group at the beginning of the tour and allow questions before parents saw the building. Apprehensive parents were all over the map with their pent-up concerns—some came armed with a robust list of "school tour questions every parent should ask;" some had personal concerns about admissions, allergies, gifted programs, discipline, uniforms, twins, test scores, or busing; and still others were openly antagonistic, hoping to prove to spouses (or themselves) that they were "on top on the situation."

If controlling or anxious parents tried to subvert the planned order with impromptu questions, the practiced parent leader would recite gently: "You know, we could talk about test scores from now until the end of time, but trust me—when you see the teachers in action, you'll experience the real thing. Let's look at the school first, and then afterward, we'll sit down with the principal and talk about the real meat-and-potatoes issues and answer any additional questions you have at that time." Prospective parents needed to experience Nettelhorst in a planned, logical progression that revealed the school's infrastructure and creative approach to learning first, followed by a tactical discussion about academia and admissions.

Prospective parents were reassured when they learned that their school visit was not a one-shot deal. Before parents entered the first classroom, the leader would announce that they were welcome to come back to Nettelhorst any day to observe classes and ask more questions. If parents wanted to sit in on a third-grade class or a preschool class for a week, it was fine with the school; they simply needed to call the office to arrange it. What they would see on the tour would be no different than what they would see any other day. The possibility of future access, an anomaly in any school, would go a long way toward ratcheting down tensions.

A small tour also gave prospective parents the opportunity to connect with other neighborhood parents. The intimate peer setting allowed parents to voice issues that might be considered embarrassing or impolitic to address within a larger audience, specifically fears that Nettelhorst was dangerous or academically unsound. In the intimacy of a small weekly tour, a parent might feel comfortable enough to admit that he feared that his toddler could not walk up the stairs without him. The whole group could stop to watch preschoolers walk up and down the stairs, holding onto the railing, with a teacher at the front and the back of the line. If a parent admitted that she was afraid that the bused-in population was "a bunch of gangbangers," the whole group could stop to watch Nettelhorst's upper-grade students gently read to preschoolers in a supervised buddy program. In a small group, nervous parents could openly question if the school would really deliver on promises beyond a pretty paint job. As parents admired the murals, the whole group could stop in the hallway to observe teachers, parents, or community volunteers instructing small groups of students clearly reading above grade level. The small size of the weekly tour gave prospective parents the security to be insecure, enabling them to ask what was really on their minds.

On a parent-led tour, the leader could linger in the classrooms of the most qualified teachers. As Nettelhorst's first open house made painfully clear, even the school's most competent teachers were hard-pressed to explain their educational philosophy and teaching methods in front of a large group of strangers. But when teachers were safely ensconced in their own classrooms, they were quite capable of describing what their students were doing at that particular moment, without the fear that the principal was evaluating them or that their peers were judging them. A parent-led tour allowed Nettelhorst's best teachers to shine.

The marketing team suspected that most prospective parents would form their impression of Nettelhorst based on their tour experience and their personal affinity for the tour guide, in much the same way parents and students evaluated possible college choices: If the high school senior believed that his tour guide was cool, surely the college would be filled with fun, interesting students; if the parents thought the guide was poised, intelligent, and articulate, clearly the school offered a quality education. If the Nettelhorst tour guide was a neighborhood mom from similar circumstances and not a school employee touting the party line, parents would likely trust her assessment of the school. If her family had other school options but still concluded that Nettelhorst was good enough for her own children, her endorsement would speak volumes. In short, the parent tour guide was not only selling the school, she was selling herself. While prospective parents might doubt that Nettelhorst would ever become a viable choice, even the most risk-averse parents could respect the co-op parent's honesty, enthusiasm, and willingness to invest with her own children.

Before the principal joined the tour to answer academic questions, the parent leader could also offer firsthand knowledge of Susan's abilities. Prospective parents were often amazed that the front office handled so many school tasks simultaneously, and sometimes they were put off by the staff's never-ending three-ring juggling act. The leader admitted that public school wasn't for the fainthearted, and Nettelhorst had a long way to travel before its customer service would match the hype. The school was still in the exciting groundbreaking stages of fulfilling its vision, and one should not expect perfectly smooth sailing yet.

Moreover, the job of leading any public school was complex, and Nettelhorst's principal wasn't perfect. The parent leader assured prospective parents that Susan's superior traits as an educator far outweighed any apparent shortcomings. One only had to look around her office to know that she was passionate about children. Her office bookshelves were filled, not with sterile bureaucratic manuals but with artwork, mementos from her students, and children's toys gathered from a lifetime of travels throughout the world. If Susan was late for a scheduled meeting, her tardiness was likely caused by her predilection to stop everything to teach a child an important lesson, such as how to walk down the stairs safely, read a difficult sentence, or find a lost ballet slipper. The reformers had all taken this risk of faith because they believed that Susan's insight and passion would trump anything else.

After the parent-led portion of the tour, Susan would join the group to assuage prospective parents' concerns, and would stay to answer questions as long as parents asked them; visitors who arrived at Nettelhorst for story time at nine in the morning might not leave until noon, and frequently, conversations between prospective parents would continue on the school's playground afterward. Given that Nettelhorst's reformation in the 1970s unraveled despite everyone's best efforts, prospective parents wanted to know what would keep the new movement from backsliding again. How could the school prevent a few defections from turning into another mass exodus? Would reform measures continue if and when the original co-op reformers moved on? What would prevent a new administration from undoing all the parents' progressive work?

Susan would assure them that Nettelhorst was trying to formalize as many relationships as it could so that reform measures would stick, but there wouldn't be any challenge that the school couldn't overcome if parents were willing to invest with their own children.

Most prospective parents were dubious about whether Nettelhorst's teachers could provide quality instruction, given the constraints of public school. In response to parents' fear of teacher strikes, Susan insisted that the rolling strikes that contributed to the unraveling of the 1970s reform movement were history. When the mayor gained control of the school board, most of the teachers union/school board battles that once plagued the system effectively ground to a halt. If parents asked about untenable teachers, Susan responded with as much candor as she had with co-op parents: Although Nettelhorst had many teachers who were stellar, it had some who were not performing at the level she expected. Nettelhorst might be a leap of faith, but if neighborhood parents invested with their own children, either her teachers would rise to the occasion or they could be pressured to find another school.

When unpopular policy changes hit the park rumor mill, prospective parents were particularly dubious that CPS would really tolerate local control or support up-and-coming schools. Such a challenge arose when CPS caught parents and schools unawares when it announced that the TBP program would raise tuition and cut back services citywide. Middle-class families who were finally testing the public school waters successfully pressured the board to back down, but the TBP backlash reverberated across the city. Prospective parents feared that if they committed to Nettelhorst in kindergarten, and then CPS changed the paradigm down the road, it would be difficult, if not impossible, to gain admission to another school.

During the TBP crisis, it not only became clear that public school wasn't for the timid, but the incident proved that Nettelhorst's involved parent base could quickly mount a successful defense when needed. In response to the conflict, the Co-op offered the board a position statement, accompanied by hours of videotaped Nettelhorst parent testimonials. Not only did CPS resolve the crisis by adopting many of the parents' key arguments, the defense showed that they didn't need to shout to have their voices heard downtown.

While it was one thing to convince prospective parents that Nettelhorst could circle the wagons against any external adversity, it was quite another thing to defend the school against its self-generated problems. For example, when inclusion situations failed at Nettelhorst, they did so spectacularly. If an inclusion student dominated a classroom teacher's attention or threatened other teachers or students, affected parents would resort to public venting if they felt that the school was unresponsive. During these difficult times, Susan would spend extra time on the tour patiently explaining CPS protocol and confidentiality issues to extra-nervous prospective parents.

## SPIN

Whatever the Co-op's internal differences may have been, the core group was careful to never air dirty laundry in public. The urgency of the project superseded anyone's bruised ego, and parents became adept at readily shifting between public and private personas. Within the core group, parents did not need to sugarcoat opinions (although perhaps a little more sensitivity would have been welcome); outside of the core group, parents were relentlessly upbeat: "Hey, guess what we just got!" "Did you hear that Nettelhorst is becoming a professional development center for teachers?" "Did you see that great article in the neighborhood weekly?" In public, the reform movement was always making slow but steady progress.

Why did parents need to put on such a brave face when the public clearly didn't want to hear any more lies about school reform? It was a classic chicken-and-egg dilemma: Nettelhorst needed to reach a tipping point to turn the corner, but it couldn't genuinely improve unless the neighborhood invested in force, yet the neighborhood wouldn't invest unless the school seemed to be genuinely improving. And the school wasn't going to improve unless reformers had the freedom to speak candidly about what needed to be fixed. They knew that the informal social network of the playground extended well beyond Roscoe Park; even the slightest whiff that the project was unraveling could have easily stoked a citywide rumor mill.

## INTERNAL COMMUNICATION

Given Nettelhorst's concentric circles of influence, Susan desperately needed to improve how the administration, and even how the teachers, communicated with current Nettelhorst parents. Small misunderstandings tended to get blown way out of proportion. For example, when the administration decided that teachers should bring kindergarteners into the building without their parents in tow, the school needed to clarify its new policy in a manner that would be sensitive to its new clientele.

Here, the administration learned an important lesson—to clarify motivations. Without understanding that the goal was to foster the kindergartners' independence and to speed up the drop-off process, parents jumped to the conclusion that the school didn't care about their children's emotional or physical well-being. Believing that their children were being ripped away heartlessly, and then were not being supervised well on the staircase leading to the preschool room, the parents' anger and concern began to fester on the school playground. When distraught parents asked teachers to justify Nettelhorst's new drop-off policy, teachers improvised and redirected parents to "take it up with the principal." Without a cohesive explanation from the teachers, parents looked at their sobbing five-year-olds and imagined the worst.

The lack of a consistent party line pointed out another lesson: *It is critical to take action promptly when a miscommunication occurs.* Although the parents witnessed that their children were perfectly capable of waving goodbye independently and that teachers could manage to bring them up the stairs without incident, they needed additional reassurances. The school had not banked enough goodwill to issue what appeared on the surface to be draconian policies, even though they might be the norm at other schools. As a whole, the school would need to coddle parents until it earned their trust and respect.

Most assuredly, if a pebble dropped in the waters of Nettelhorst's TBP, the ripple effect could be felt in a playground clear across town. A case in point was when the school dismissed a TBP teacher, the letter sent home to parents did not adequately explain the circumstances for the dismissal, and rumors began to travel through Chicago's parent community like a game of telephone gone wild. By the time the information found its way to the NPN chat board, the Internet presence for a well-organized parents network in Chicago, Nettelhorst was reportedly in danger of losing its TBP program entirely, which only signaled to prospective parents that the reform movement was in trouble.

To improve the communications, the marketing team made multiple recommendations. Although the actions were relatively simple, the changes resonated with the school community. First, *the school needed to alter its approach*. Memos from the principal needed to lose their institutional feel and be more in line with the peppier, personable messages coming out of the neighborhood's private schools. For example, "Dear parents/guardians" gave way to "Dear Nettelhorst families"; "Sincerely" became "All the best!" or "Have a great weekend!" Stern edicts eased to gentle reminders and loving suggestions. When the staff complained that it didn't have time to sugarcoat memos, Susan was more than happy to turn the job over to co-op parents who, thanks to e-mail, could write during their own time and send the content to her ready for editing, printing, and distributing.

Second, *the school needed to address the appearance of its communications*. The school wanted to signal a change on all levels, and what easier way to do so than through a fresh look and feel? The marketing team designed new stationery and a logo for the school to add professionalism to its correspondence. The team also suggested the school stop "doctoring up" communications with clip art and bubble fonts. Softer-hued copy paper cost the same as white or neon and would be far more pleasing to the new clientele.

Some critics might see these extra measures as inconsequential fluff, but when the school improved its correspondence to a more warm, courteous, and professional style of communication, current and prospective parents took notice and became more confident that Nettelhorst was on par with the other schools in the neighborhood. In time, parent volunteers would expand and refine the school's internal communication: Janet Peterson created an annual school directory (a huge task given CPS confidentiality issues), Holly Quasny sent regular school-wide e-mail blasts, Florence Powdermaker wrote a monthly newsletter, and Rachel Switall supervised a quarterly student-written magazine. But in the early days of the reform movement, a well-presented photocopied communication was worlds ahead of the school's usual fare.

## PUBLIC RELATIONS

While the marketing team hoped to reach the families with young children who lived within the school's immediate neighborhood, Nettelhorst hoped to extend its campaign to other neighborhoods. Families who were unhappy with their own neighborhood school, locked out of private schools, or unlucky in the magnet lottery might be willing to drive their kids to Nettelhorst or even move into the district. Nettelhorst took its rag-tag dog and pony show to any neighborhood organization, church, synagogue, retirement home, or condominium board that would listen. The message was always the same: Nettelhorst desperately wanted to become the heart of the community, but the school could not do it alone. Even if neighbors did not have children, they could help the school by coming to the weekly farmers' market, attending a community event, volunteering to tutor students, or lending their professional expertise. Even if listeners never set foot in Nettelhorst, they could still help the school by broadcasting the reformers' story to the city at large.

Until neighborhood families bought in with their own children, reformers believed that poaching students from other neighborhoods would be a reasonable quick fix. Like all underutilized neighborhood magnet schools, Nettelhorst could choose to boost attendance by enrolling students who lived outside the attendance boundary. While CPS certainly would have preferred that Nettelhorst draw students from within the school's boundary, until neighborhood families decided to invest, the school was free to enroll children from other neighborhoods. Consequently, if reformers convinced enough non-neighborhood, middle-class families to enroll their children, neighborhood families might be enticed, and the school might reach a tipping point.

While the nascent reform movement was a compelling story, media coverage tended to focus on Chicago's most dangerous or highest performing schools, and the Co-op's PR team found it virtually impossible to generate any interest. All that changed when Rickey Gold & Associates, a small, local public relations firm, volunteered to help Nettelhorst navigate the media waters. Rickey constantly fed her media contacts different angles, hoping the school would find traction. For example, if Rickey heard that a food columnist was writing a story about winter casseroles, she would try to entice them with a recipe from Nettelhorst students. As soon as Rickey was briefed on the latest Nettelhorst news, she would issue a press release or copy-ready stories. Every time Nettelhorst received coverage, however small, the school gained legitimacy.

As the reform movement gained speed, Rickey pressed the school to become more media savvy. While increased exposure would drive enrollment, no one seemed to grasp the reality that Nettelhorst was in danger of being closed (even as CPS cut positions and shuttered neighboring schools). Consequently, most staff members made for begrudging PR students. Before every planned media visit, the staff bristled at the intrusion—the maintenance staff resented the extra scrutiny and frenzied need to clean up for company, the security guard hated being restricted to monitoring the front door, and the teaching staff believed every dog and pony show interrupted the business of teaching and learning. Only Nettelhorst students seemed to relish the increased media attention.

Even if staff members couldn't understand Rickey's motivations, her professional reputation was on the line each and every time she issued a press release on the school's behalf. If reporters had a bad experience at Nettelhorst, not only would they not come back in the future, they might not take Rickey seriously when she promoted her own paying clients. She encouraged the school to formalize its PR strategy. Every student was asked to sign a media release that would be in effect for the full school year. High-profile school events needed to follow carefully planned agendas. Rickey did not have time to dillydally with the school office or CPS bureaucracy; reporters had deadlines and egos that required the school to be responsive and nimble. Heart warming public school fluff was not deep investigative journalism; the school needed to make it easy for reporters to get in, get their story, and get out. Nettel- horst also needed to build long-term media relationships. If the school treated reporters kindly and responsively, the media would return when- ever it required a public school angle.

Could parent volunteers run a successful public relations campaign without professional expertise? Possibly. While the school never would have had the time to e-mail press releases and make follow-up calls, par- ent volunteers could certainly follow a simple PR rubric and do much of the actual logistics from home. Parents could also help make sure the school was camera-ready and chaperone visitors without a principal's constant supervision. However, reformers learned that a successful pub- lic relations campaign hinges on cultivating long-term relationships, a process that is complicated, time-consuming, and best left to experts. Years later, Nettelhorst parents Shawn Malay and Barri Leiner, both savvy public relations experts, arrived on the scene to help the school navigate the media waters, but early reformers were exceedingly lucky that Rickey adopted their fledgling cause when the school had very lit- tle to sell.

In the beginning of their journey, the Roscoe Park Eight were mys- tified as to why local newspapers repeatedly showcased the city's handful of "golden" magnet schools. As the reform movement progressed, it became clear that luck certainly played a part, but these schools had successfully crafted their own story and developed the right relationships to help promote it. No one knew how exactly Nettelhorst's story would read, but it needed to start with "one of the worst" and end with "one of the best." The neighborhood already knew the background story: By almost every measure, Nettelhorst was a lost cause. Nettelhorst was a perfect "before" snapshot of a public school—dismal test scores, disgruntled teachers, unengaged parents, and a dreary facility abandoned by neighborhood families and scorned by local business owners, politicians, and community groups. Two years into the new principal's leadership, Nettelhorst had transformed into a fairly typical Chicago public school, and yet neighborhood parents steadfastly refused to enroll their children.

*The story had to change.* Nettelhorst's new story began as a myth, fabricated out of truths, half-truths, wishful thinking, and salvaged history from the school's glory days. Every co-op team desperately needed the media's positive endorsement to gain traction. Media attention would help prove that Nettelhorst was on the up-and-up, give politicians evidence that they were serving their constituents, help CPS make its case that the system was not beyond repair, and give funders some assurance that they had backed a winner. Until the school could control its own image, reformers would be powerless to change public perception.

To be sure, the co-op marketing team's ability to rebrand and reposition Nettelhorst was impressive, but it was not really rocket science. Except for the singular fact that neighborhood parents led the reform movement, the team worked with garden-variety public school material. Certainly, Rickey hustled to get Nettelhorst play, but to some degree a public school success story sells itself. The actual spin was really not all that remarkable; what was notable, however, was the speed and extent to which Nettelhorst's vision became self-fulfilling. No one could have predicted that the hype would become such a powerful catalyst for internal change.

## WHEN GOOD ENOUGH IS NOT ENOUGH

Thanks to everyone's hard work, Nettelhorst seemed ready to sprint from the gate, yet many families were unwilling to take a risk on what the school might become *someday*. One prospective parent put it quite bluntly: "You can take Spam, gussy it up, and call it pâté," he warned, "but at the end of the day, if it is still Spam, we're not eating." Nettelhorst might be a noble social experiment—a vision of what American education could and should be—but for some, it was safer to walk away from the table before the school could even serve the meal. Quite simply, many park parents could never see beyond the school's earliest incarnation. They simply knew too much—the low scores, the unruly students, the underperforming teachers, the administration's history of incompetence, and the Co-op's smoke and mirrors. Many park parents grew weary of all the Nettelhorst hype day after day and grew tired of the constant begging and proselytizing. Finding the right elementary school was supposed to be, well, elementary. Surely the path was less painful somewhere—*anywhere*—else.

The Roscoe Park Eight had given the movement every ounce of their energy and needed to accept the hard truth that some parents—even some who were the most active participants—would inevitably decide to send their children elsewhere. It is telling that all the parents on the Co-op's original curriculum team opted to enroll their own children in private schools or selective magnet schools. Despite all their efforts to change the school and the progress they were beginning to make, the curriculum team parents had seen more than enough. No amount of marketing spin could shake their memory of a Nettelhorst teacher swearing at a child or students harassing community residents walking down the school's sidewalk.

Many core reformers who did not have access to the curriculum team's privileged information found the leap of faith too much to bear. For example, a core reformer who had devoted hundreds of hours to transforming Nettelhorst pulled her daughter from the TBP program after her very first week of preschool. How was it, she wondered, that she could hold down a full-time job, raise two kids under three, and still manage to find the time to personally unpack and set up the preschool classroom's furniture (delivered a mere week before school began), yet the teacher could not find the time to do something as simple as write her daughter's name on the school cubby. Was it too much to ask a preschool teacher to personalize a child's very first school experience?

If her child had enrolled in a private preschool instead of Nettelhorst, she reasoned, her new teacher would have sent a personal letter during the summer with a roster of classmates to facilitate introductions and arrange early playdates. The school would have hosted an open house before school started so that children could meet their new teacher and classmates and see the classroom. On the first day of school, her daughter would have found her cubby with ease, because it would have been distinguished by her block-printed name and her own smiling photograph. Private school tuition might bankrupt her family, but at least she could be sure that her kid would get individualized attention. The straw that finally broke the camel's back, for this parent, was the lack of a cubby nameplate.

Beyond the personal sting, reformers knew that every defection could jeopardize the entire movement. In an initial preschool class of forty students, split between two classrooms, the loss of just a few families could inspire a mass exodus, which is exactly what prompted the school's downward spiral in the seventies. To make matters worse, the heavily subsidized TBP model was only solvent if each preschool maintained full enrollment, and the cash-strapped board had threatened to close any TBP that dipped below eighteen students. If the preschool lost just three families, Nettelhorst might lose its TBP program altogether, middle-class neighborhood families would no longer have a low-risk way to test the waters, and the entire reform movement could be undone.

Every time a neighborhood family gave up on Nettelhorst, the Roscoe Park Eight blamed the school for failing to anticipate the specific needs of its new middle-class clientele. Susan wondered what more neighborhood families expected her to do—she had quietly honored classroom teacher or friendship requests; she spent hours and hours reassuring nervous parents that the school would be responsive to their needs; she hosted an ice cream social the week before school started so that students could see their classrooms and meet their teachers; on the first day of school, she hosted a catered "Butterfly Breakfast" so that new preschool and kindergarten parents would have a gentle transition; she even had the fire department send a truck over on the first day so that firemen could greet children as they arrived. All these activities were designed to make parents and children comfortable with their school choice—and all of them went beyond any board requirements.

If the new middle-class neighborhood parents wanted a seat at the table, it couldn't be a booster chair; Nettelhorst was public school, not a romper room. If parents received only one mailing over the summer, it was because Nettelhorst had enough money for only one stamp. The school couldn't send student rosters because of confidentiality issues, and the before-school open house seemed dinky because the teachers, by union contract, weren't required to return (even to set up their class-rooms) until one day before school started. If the school felt strapped and understaffed, it was because it *was* strapped and understaffed. If par-ents wanted someone to answer the school's telephone during the sum-mer, they would have to figure out a way to obtain a voice mail system for free or find a volunteer to sit at the clerk's desk. Susan could not be a principal and a receptionist simultaneously (although she spent a good part of the summer answering the phone). The reality was that this was still a public school—if the new parents wanted more, they needed to step up and help in the effort.

Susan's point was well-taken, but prospective parents could hardly be expected to grab an oar and start rowing before they even got on the boat. Many parents saw Nettelhorst as a third- or fourth-tier backup school, but they still needed to do due diligence; parents of preschool-ers needed to formally apply to the school's TBP program, even if they were just hedging their bets. Unfortunately, the surging interest from neighborhood parents caught everyone by surprise, and callers heard contradictory information from whoever happened to pick up the office phone. To make matters worse, Nettelhorst had never bothered to establish any formal mechanism for processing incoming applications. CPS had left each school free to develop and manage its own TBP admissions policy, and Nettelhorst processed so few applications that if a child was three years old, potty-trained, and breathing, he could join the class.

When the school hastily cobbled together a formal TBP admissions policy, prospective parents became irate when the queue numbers scribbled on their applications bore absolutely no correlation to whose children were being accepted. The administration struggled to balance classes by gender, age, and residency, while simultaneously trying to honor assurances that sweat equity would guarantee a child's spot in preschool. Compounding matters still, many neighborhood parents were only hedging their bets by applying to Nettelhorst's TBP, and the school had led them to believe that deposits would be refundable. However, as the process unfolded, it became clear that the school had no way of returning deposits once they had been submitted to the board. Neighborhood parents were furious, Susan was besieged with complaints, and reformers were challenged to put on a brave face.

In truth, reformers also contributed to the school's early enrollment woes. When co-op parents offered to help the school create a rubric for TBP admissions, the seemingly capable parent volunteer in charge of overseeing the project created a firestorm. Not only had his own child's out-of-district TBP application miraculously jumped to the front of the wait-list, but many parents who had been offered verbal acceptance several months earlier suddenly found their children rejected, just weeks before school was to begin. By the time the school discovered what had happened, the acceptance letters had all been mailed, families had accepted and registered, and the damage could not be undone. To remedy this disastrous situation, Susan made house calls to spurned, prospective TBP parents, apologizing for the bungled applications. She begged them to consider reapplying to the TBP the following year and promised to chaperone their applications personally. When a prospective parent called the school to say that she was giving up after the school gave her the wrong TBP application to fill out (twice!), Susan drove to her house with the correct forms to sign.

Finally, the school's very gifted counselor took charge of TBP admissions and the process improved immediately, but it still wasn't smooth sailing. The counselor didn't have time to do her job *and* coddle nervous, prospective parents. Neighborhood parents, who already felt the need to chaperone their child's applications at established magnet schools, heard that Nettelhorst's applications needed extra-special attention. The counselor simply did not have enough time in the day to return the hundreds of calls each month from prospective parents who were "just checking in" to see where their precious darling ranked on the school's TBP wait-list. Eventually, a pro bono web designer would create an informative school website that would answer at least the most basic admissions questions, but until then, the school worked overtime to provide customer service to its demanding new clientele.

Even when the school formalized its admissions policy, if prospective parents didn't really believe that Nettelhorst was *good enough*, extra somersaults and cartwheels weren't going to change their minds. When the school stumbled one too many times, prospective parents would likely phone Jacqueline to break the news that they had decided to enroll their child elsewhere. She tried to put on a brave face when hearing the news and wished them well, but inside, she was crushed. Everyone had poured so much energy into recruiting and catering to individual families; the fact that their efforts proved insufficient cut deeply.

Worse yet, what if the deserters were right? What if the reformers had been drinking the doctored Nettelhorst punch for so long that they could no longer distinguish fact from fiction? Each departure would inevitably force the Roscoe Park Eight to revisit sobering conversations about Nettelhorst's viability, and each time, Susan would ride circuit around the neighborhood to reassure core families that her school would deliver.

Whereas the core group saw every family that went AWOL as a sign of Nettelhorst's failure, Susan believed that it was more the parents' failure to not stay with a relationship through thick and thin. She argued that when something goes wrong, if disenchanted parents pull their children from a school in a huff, they inadvertently teach their children that the appropriate response to losing is to overturn the board game. Children would have the opportunity to learn responsibility if they observed adults actively solving problems rather than running from them. If the process of creating great schools was easy, Susan argued, every school would be great. Change required determination and persistence. Parents needed to strap on seatbelts for the bumpy ride, trusting that, in the end, the school community would make the situation work.

As Susan bent over backward to calm apprehensive parents, her most loyal and sympathetic staff members wanted their principal to get back to the business of running a school. The parents rejected all attempts to curb their access. Once the clerk tried in vain to limit access, posting an "ONLY OFFICE PERSONNEL ALLOWED" sign on the principal's office door, but the Co-op promptly removed the sign because it sent the "wrong message" to prospective parents.

Just as parents had little understanding of how much havoc their actions caused within the school, Susan's staff could barely comprehend how many unpaid, overworked volunteers were laboring on Nettelhorst's behalf. As most of the core parents had babies and toddlers at home, the cost of volunteering, particularly in an endeavor without social standing or assurances of success, was extremely high. Stay-at-home parents multitasked and worked during nap times or late into the night. Working parents split their time among family obligations, work, and volunteering at the school, often leading to strain in whichever area was being most overlooked at any given point. As self-imposed deadlines approached, disagreements sometimes devolved into tears or escalated into shouting matches. Co-op volunteers seemed to require an endless degree of validation.

Key staff members argued that Nettelhorst simply didn't have enough time or energy to grow hothouse orchids through a blizzard. If these entitled, latte-swilling, yuppie parents didn't think that public school in general, or Nettelhorst in particular, was already good enough for their overindulged offspring, who needed them? Nettelhorst would surely disappoint at some point down the road, and then they would cut and run. Wouldn't the school be better off, these teachers pondered, directing its limited energy toward families who had already committed, rather than chasing after elusive neighborhood prima donnas?

While neighborhood parents might seem needy or aloof, Susan suggested that they were likely hardier that those found in other gentrified Chicago neighborhoods. East Lakeview/Boystown wasn't known for being particularly "family friendly." Few restaurants offered children's menus or crayons, the only toy store went out of business, and the local theater booked shows like *The Marijuanalogues* and *The Puppetry of the Penis*.

As more and more parents decided to raise children in the city, many Chicagoans bristled as negligent parents encroached on their "child-free" turf. The conflict went national on the front page of the *New York Times* when a trendy café posted a sign in the window saying, "Children of all ages have to behave and use their indoor voices when coming to A Taste of Heaven."[7] Although the ensuing boycott was largely overblown, the sign uncovered a raw nerve in the city's ongoing mommy wars.

The Taste of Heaven flap took on its own incarnation in East Lakeview/Boystown. Some longtime residents blamed the arrival of middle-class parents for the neighborhood's skyrocketing real estate prices and ever increasing congestion. Still others blamed the "breeders," with their cell phones and battering-ram double strollers, for eroding the neighborhood's grit and character. However, most neighbors, gay and straight, were willing to live and let live. Tolerance cut both ways: Stroller moms needed to share the sidewalk with a diverse segment of society—goth-punks, openly gay couples, panhandlers, buskers, Cubs fans, Krishnas, Orthodox Jews, and Lake Shore Drive socialites. Needless to say, in a neighborhood where transvestite waiters were the norm, the neighborhood school would tend to attract a more free-spirited, liberal brand of parent.

Even if the new arrivals turned out to be the stereotypical, high-maintenance types, they needed to be accepted as part and parcel of a larger social umbrella. When a Nettelhorst mother initiated a public crusade to close a newly opened, upscale sex shop, Susan responded by walking over to the store after school one afternoon, introducing herself as the principal of Nettelhorst, and welcoming the owner to the neighborhood.[8] On Sunday evenings, The Righteously Outrageous Twirling Corps (ROTC), an all-male group known for its flirtatious precision rifle routines set to disco songs, practiced a PG version in the school's front playlot. On the day of the Gay and Lesbian Pride Parade, Nettelhorst's marquee read, "At Nettelhorst, we believe family means everybody." The news of Susan's commitment to the Boystown residents spread rapidly throughout the neighborhood.[9] She firmly believed that Nettelhorst could only succeed if it embraced the entire community—in all its colorful permutations.

While some staff members may have bought into the argument that these early adopters were a progressive group of women, it was all too likely that parents who were less risk-tolerant would ultimately buy-in. If the first wave of neighborhood parents seemed like hot house orchids in a blizzard, subsequent waves would surely be even higher maintenance. It wouldn't be long before Nettelhorst's disadvantaged minority student body would be replaced by a more sanitized kind of diversity. While Susan shared some of her staff's fears, she accepted that the larger forces of gentrification were unstoppable; chain coffee shops and video stores were a reality of urban renewal. However, if Lakeview's middle-class parents were really elitist or xenophobic, surely other neighborhoods and other neighborhood schools would present a better fit. Just as park parents needed to let go of some of their biases and assumptions, her staff needed to give the incoming parents a little leeway.

Whenever neighborhood parents appeared to be losing faith in Nettelhorst's ability to turn the corner, Susan would advise them that the grass would not be greener elsewhere. Another school might answer the phone or open the front door more promptly, it might even have the stamps to send out fabulously descriptive, color-coded informational packets, but it would inevitably suffer from other deep-rooted problems. All schools, even the most expensive private or selective public schools, inevitably had some lunatic parents, problematic children, poor teachers, or any combination thereof. Schools were nothing more than teams of people working together to educate children. People were fallible; ergo, all schools were fallible.

While no school would ever be perfect, great schools exist simply because the people involved in them demand greatness and are willing to participate in the process of making them great. No one needed to descend from on high bearing a gifted program or special status to make Nettelhorst a viable school. Parents already had all the resources in front of them to make the school into the kind of place they wanted it to be. They just had to open their hearts and minds and start working. But, as with any relationship worth its salt, everyone needed patience and faith.

When jittery parents began to wonder whether private school really was a better option, Susan always reassured them that public school was a reasonable choice. The reformers' children would flourish at Nettelhorst for the same reasons that they thrived at home: When children feel loved, respected, and cared for, they have the courage to learn and take risks. Private schools didn't have a monopoly on care. She spoke from personal experience; her own daughter had attended one of Chicago's top private schools, and while it offered her a fine education, it wasn't the best fit because her daughter didn't feel at home. Private schools might have more resources and look more enticing, but they were not necessarily filled with more competent teachers or even more intelligent children.

Private school parents didn't love their children any more than pubic school parents loved theirs. In fact, parents who paid exorbitant tuition oftentimes felt exempt from hands-on school responsibilities, believing that parental involvement meant idling in the morning drop-off queue or writing a check for the school's fundraiser. There was simply no substitute for a parent's active presence in their child's school life any more than in his or her home life. Neighborhood children would have just as reasonable a shot at happiness and academic success at Nettelhorst as they would at any private school because they would benefit from their parents' love, support, and most importantly, their presence.

Unlike most principals in the city, either at public or private schools, Susan promised prospective parents unfettered classroom access. Because not all children relished their parents' presence during school, or vice versa, she welcomed parents to volunteer in any other classroom. As the young parents had scarcely an idea of how involved they would want to be, or even should be, in their child's academic life, this open invitation was intoxicating. Working parents were reassured to know other parents could help "mind the store" in their absence. Nettelhorst might set some boundaries down the line, but for the time being, more hands on deck could only help. A strong parental presence would also benefit the children whose parents were only marginally involved in the school: Care would always read as care. Susan insisted that when any parent acted to improve the school environment, all the students would take notice.

Ultimately, all the Co-op's fancy packaging, spin, and clever ploys would have crashed and burned if neighborhood parents believed that Susan was lying; unfettered parental access guaranteed that she was not. Smoke and mirrors might have helped deliver prospective parents to Nettelhorst's front door, but from the moment they walked in, the school needed to hold up under scrutiny. And it did.

# SIX

# FUNDRAISING

## LOOK BEYOND A
## CLIMATE OF CARE

REMEMBERING the naysayer in the park who had prophe-
sized that Susan only wanted to boost enrollment in order to
augment her dwindling budget, the Roscoe Park Eight imagined that once Nettelhorst bustled with neighborhood children, the
school's financial woes would be solved. Ironically, their very success
populating the school with neighborhood children managed to drain
the school's coffers, systematically. Of course, Nettelhorst was hardly
singing a new song: The underfunding of public education is a national
epidemic.

In Illinois, a state that boasts the remarkable distinction of ranking
second to last in the nation for state educational funding, many public
schools feel compelled to turn to private fundraising efforts to shore up
the increasingly wider gaps in public funding. Unfortunately, very few
public schools—even high-performing and well-attended schools—have
the energy or expertise to raise significant funds on their own. Consequently, most principals make do with the limited funds they receive
from the board plus the meager earnings their Parent Teacher Associa-

tion (PTA) might raise at bake sales, ticket raffles, car washes, and the like. In Chicago and across the nation, a very select group of public school principals, on top of all their other titles, have managed to become rainmakers as well, bringing in hundreds of thousands of dollars each year from private donors.

While Susan appreciated that Nettelhorst needed to raise significant funds, she was reticent to inflame racial and socioeconomic tensions within the school community. Any serious fundraising effort could have unintended but serious repercussions on the fragile state of the reform movement. If some of Nettelhorst's teachers and parents already felt threatened by the new yuppie neighborhood parents, what would they think of a fancy party and silent auction that targeted the largess of a few, predominantly white families? After the first year, reformers proposed that the school was ready to host a silent auction, betting that there were now enough middle-class families with kindergarten and TBP students to support it. Susan rejected the idea outright. A twenty-dollar beer night at a local bar was no different than a hundred-dollar dinner at a fancy restaurant. The problem didn't lie in the event's price point; rather, *any* fundraising event that took place off of school property would inevitably lead to charges of elitism. Whatever revenue a party might generate for the school simply wasn't worth the risk of imperiling the movement.

Even if Susan had overestimated the threat of internal backlash, reformers agreed to put fundraising on the back burner. Reformers were having considerable success revitalizing Nettelhorst without tapping into the financial resources of community members or the school's current parents—or digging into their own pockets. All the co-op teams had managed to reach their goals without spending a dime. The infrastructure team renovated the school by soliciting goods and services from neighborhood merchants; the special events team made Nettelhorst the heart of the neighborhood by outsourcing a weekly farmers' market and annual community events; the marketing team enticed prospective parents by creating a forward-thinking campaign—all pro bono; and the enrichment team secured a $300,000 grant to seed the innovative, self-sustaining community school. Not bad for a group of eight moms and their teams of volunteers!

Even if fundraising were an option, it is doubtful that early reformers would have the energy or expertise to launch a more serious effort at that particular time. The Roscoe Park parents knew of only one skilled grant writer in the neighborhood, park mom Eileen Swartout, and she had already invested all her efforts into writing the community school's grant with Hull House while simultaneously raising three children under five. Even though reformers had managed to secure annual memberships to Donors Forum, an Illinois clearinghouse of grants for the not-for-profit community, neither the Co-op nor the school had the capacity to apply for the grants.

Because none of the other park parents had any fundraising experience at all, the Co-op tried to solicit a professional fundraiser to help the cause. However, no one was willing to work for free, and everyone insisted on being paid upfront or on retainer. Most reformers couldn't abide the idea of paying someone when everyone else was working around the clock gratis. Even if they had found someone willing to work on commission, it seemed unseemly (if not unethical) to ask the school to part with any potential grant winnings. In light of these limitations, reformers resolved to keep moving forward, one donated gallon of paint at a time.

While everyone would have loved more resources, the school seemed to be making do. It rented out the teachers' parking lot to neighborhood residents after hours and on the weekends, earning almost $20,000 in unrestricted funds each year. Plus, a few thousand dollars were netted each year through Friends of Nettelhorst (FON) from traditional bake sales, holiday candy and wrapping paper sales, and so forth. Together, the additional funds from FON and the parking lot didn't make much of a dent in the school's overall budget, but it was more "found" money compared to what most principals had at their disposal.

Susan believed that the real value of FON micro-fundraisers was not really the revenue they brought to the school, but the "climate of care" that they helped to create within the school community. A case in point:

the seasonal sales of construction paper shamrocks, tulips, or turkeys that FON would hawk during the school's bi-annual report card pickup days. She maintained that these tables helped foster a warm community spirit. When disenfranchised parents took the initiative to buy a two-dollar flower—a financial reach for many parents—to be personalized with their child's name and posted on the school wall, their child would pass the flower every day and know that their parents cared about them and Nettelhorst. The flower tangibly represented the value the parents placed on the child's education. To Susan, every single act of parental engagement, no matter how small, mattered in the eyes of a child.

This civics lesson was lost on the early reformers. When Susan insisted that overburdened co-op volunteers—who were already hosting a teacher appreciation lunch and registering students for Jane's Place classes—also man a FON micro-fundraiser table, tempers flared. Just how much free time did she think that they had? Reformers wanted to be supportive, but a full day spent cutting paper flowers seemed like an utter waste of their time and talents, given the minimal financial gain. Over the years, reformers came to understand and embrace the social value of these micro-fundraisers, but at the time, only one thing seemed clear: Financial cheerleading in two-dollar increments wasn't going to bridge the funding chasm. While the Roscoe Park parents had successfully solicited hundreds of thousands of dollars worth of in-kind goods and services to revitalize the school, they weren't in any position to scramble together the hard cash necessary to refurbish a science lab or renovate an auditorium. These kinds of large-scale projects couldn't be tackled piecemeal. The cold reality was that paper tulips weren't going to provide the sufficient funds the school needed to jump to the next level.

The need to do *something* began to mount as the school's annual operating budget had constricted each and every year. It was a curious and demoralizing state of affairs: Although CPS funding increased marginally as the school enrolled more neighborhood children, state funding decreased exponentially as the school's low-income population decreased and test scores improved. In short, Nettelhorst had become a victim of its own success. By the third year, Nettelhorst's LSC had just

$125,000 in annual discretionary income to cover all textbooks, office equipment, professional development, and nonessential salaries. Thus, if Nettelhorst needed to hire one extra teacher to avoid a split grade, the school might not be able to buy paper and pencils for the year, let alone outfit a science lab or refurbish the worn-out auditorium.

It was unclear how long Nettelhorst would be able meet to the expectations of incoming neighborhood parents with its rapidly shrinking budget. A split in the fourth/fifth grade might be tolerated for a year or two, but eventually, cutbacks would hit closer to home. All-day kindergarten would likely be the next luxury item on the chopping block. In the past, Nettelhorst could absorb the cost of all-day kindergarten (the board only provided funding for a half-day kindergarten teacher), but now that neighborhood children had arrived in force, one kindergarten classroom had ballooned into three. As much as everyone wanted all-day kindergarten, most of the school's discretionary funds were now used to fill the funding gap.

Some other neighborhood schools were turning toward their parent base to make up the funding difference. For example, when a nearby successful elementary school faced a similar crisis, the "friends of" group turned to the school's parents to pony up. In less than two weeks, the parents donated over $100,000, enough to pay for an extra teacher and save the school's all-day kindergarten. At yet another successful neighborhood school, the "friends of" group decided to stop nickel-and-diming parents with the yearly smorgasbord of small-scale fundraisers. In a novel move, it decided to ask families for an annual voluntary pledge of one thousand dollars (or any comfortable amount). In the first three months of the new direct appeal, the parents' group raised over $150,000.[1]

Despite the tremendous success these schools had raising large sums of money internally, many Nettelhorst reformers cautioned that any overt shakedown, even if confidential and voluntary, would only exacerbate socioeconomic divisions. Following the example of neighboring schools, Nettelhorst launched a similar campaign suggesting that parents donate a thousand dollars per child, or whatever amount parents felt comfortable giving. Even though organizers' promised confidentiality would be

respected, and a one-dollar donation and a one-thousand-dollar donation would be honored equally with the same hand-printed wall tile, the
parental backlash was so fierce that the school opted to suspend the campaign. And yet, it became clear that, sooner or later, Nettelhorst would
have to stop tiptoeing around the funding crisis. If parents wanted to
keep Nettelhorst's all-day kindergarten, and the state of Illinois only paid
for half-day kindergarten, the LSC could not draw from school's ever-
shrinking discretionary funds indefinitely. Something had to give.

How would Nettelhorst ever be able to respond to budgetary challenges like the kindergarten shortfall if it didn't have a credible fundraising apparatus in place? It was highly unlikely that the state or the federal
government was going to change the way public education was financed
any time soon. The cash-strapped school board was unable or unwilling
to deliver a corporate partner to help. It was folly to believe that a major
donor was going to materialize magically out of the ether. Quite simply,
Nettelhorst needed to start helping itself.

After four years of relentless pressure from the reformers and
increasing budgetary concerns, Susan agreed that the situation was dire
and allowed reformers to host a serious fundraiser. Under the FON banner, co-op moms Ellen Bakal and Tracy Wozniak and their team of
supermoms planned a wine tasting and silent auction at a swank local
wine bar. Unfortunately, just as Susan predicted, every facet of the
planned fundraising event triggered class issues, from the ticket price, to
the venue, to the fancy invitations, to the price of auction items.[2] Planners found the charges of elitism exasperating, as they had worked long
into every night to plan the event.

The workload was staggering. Before the party, planners needed to
assemble invitations, solicit and organize hundreds of donated items,
and physically get them all on site. At the party, volunteers needed to
set up the auction with appropriate bid sheets, register the guests, and
manage an expeditious checkout. And following the party, this same
group processed payments and wrote thank you/tax exemption letters
to all the donors. Moreover, reformers had managed to obtain almost
all the items needed for the entire event—including the invitations,

venue, food, alcohol, music, and the auction items—*for free*. Except for tipping the five waiters and covering incidentals, all the profits would go directly into the school's discretionary fund. If the wine tasting party didn't look or feel like an egalitarian social event, it was because it *wasn't*. Reformers wanted to be sensitive to economic disparities, but their intention was to raise money for the school—which would, in turn, benefit *everyone*.

And raise money, they did. The first time out of the gate, reformers brought in $17,000 at the one-night event, which they immediately doubled using a CPS matching grant to buy new playground equipment.[3] As soon as naysayers saw what a serious fundraising event might accomplish for the school, the grumbling stopped.

## FUNDRAISING 101

With the success of the first wine tasting and silent auction behind them, reformers were confident that the movement was solid enough to begin a fundraising effort in earnest. Again, neighborhood parents led the charge. New kindergarten parent Ted Ganchiff did not have any experience raising money for schools, per se, but he did have a professional background that made him a quick study. Ted had worked in Silicon Valley during the boom, taking a podcast company from conception through funding to rapid growth (and to just as rapid of a demise), and then moved to Chicago to start Spinforce, a communications consultancy, with his wife. Just as the original reformers inspired a community to turn a bad school into a good school, Ted imagined that the community could be inspired to turn a good school into a great school if properly motivated. Ted suspected that Nettelhorst, like any well-chaperoned start-up company, could reach its full potential if reformers changed the way they pitched for money, partnerships, and media attention.

Just as the original park parents had researched similar reform movements to get their bearings, Ted did his due diligence. Although CPS actively encouraged schools to raise funds independently, it failed (and continues to fail) to offer any development tools to aid in the process. The complex CPS website offered no explanation for how a school might set up a Friends of…organization, a completely distinct and independent, not-for-profit fundraising entity (a tax-exempt status from the Internal Revenue Service, pursuant to Section 501(c)(3) of the Internal Revenue Code). The public library wasn't proving to be much help, either. While many fundraising manuals targeted not-for-profit organizations, nothing seemed to speak directly to Nettelhorst's unique position as a middle-class, urban public school. Just as early reformers had no ready-made blueprint for how neighborhood parents might transform a bad school into a good school, Ted found no clear guide for how public schools might fundraise beyond the traditional bake sale model.

Ted wondered why CPS hadn't delivered a corporate partner to adopt the school. After all, Chicago seemed overrun by philanthropically minded corporations whose largess always seemed to be helping one public school or another. Nettelhorst never had any luck finding a corporate partner on its own, even at special times when CPS seemed to be handing them out. Nettelhorst had high hopes that CPS would send a corporate angel to adopt the school at Chicago's Principal for a Day, an event launched by Mayor Daley in 1998 that places celebrities and civic and corporate leaders in the city's public schools. As the purpose of the Principal for a Day is to encourage long-term, win-win partnerships, reformers tried every which way to make the school more enticing to a potential sponsor.

The Co-op's public relations team suspected that VIPs sent to Nettelhorst would respond well to added media attention, so the public relations team arranged for extra fanfare to surround the day. Every year, the team snagged fabulous guests to join the VIPs that CPS assigned to Nettelhorst: the Radio City Rockettes, the Food Network's Hearty Boys, and the giant BZOTs, six-foot-tall dancing and singing robots.[4] While the VIPs sent by the mayor's office and CPS enjoyed their time at the school, and even appreciated the extra sparkle that celebrity chefs, kicking Rockettes, or giant BZOTs brought to the day, their initial enthusiasm never translated into anything tangible.

Maybe Nettelhorst *was* lovable, but CPS had just sent the *wrong* VIP to Nettelhorst that morning. Maybe the *right* VIP was still floating around the Principal for a Day luncheon, just waiting to fall head over heels in love with Nettelhorst. Knowing that the ballroom was filled with vetted partners who were potentially *right* for the school, Susan and Jacqueline would work the gathering looking for someone—anyone—who might be willing to visit Nettelhorst. Surely if the *right* VIP came to visit, it would be love at first sight; then, all the school's financial troubles would be solved. Surprisingly, their gumption paid off, and after many insistent follow-up phone calls and e-mails, several CEOs did come to visit Nettelhorst. However, even after what seemed to be wildly successful tours of the school, visitors were happy to give advice or offer contacts, but no one ever wanted to formalize the relationship. Try as it might, Nettelhorst wasn't having any luck finding a corporate partner, either through its own creative efforts or through any formal CPS channel.

If CPS had no intention of delivering a corporate angel or even a fundraising bible to help Nettelhorst, maybe parents from one of Chicago's "golden" schools could help Ted develop a strategy. Early on, golden school parents were quick to share what made their schools so successful, but now it seemed as though no one was talking. Parents at other schools were unwilling to share even the rudimentary mechanics of how to run a silent auction, create an alumni database, secure not-for-profit status, and so on. The stonewalling appeared to be a defensive strategy. Just as neighboring schools failed to release their TBP overflow students to help fill Nettelhorst's struggling TBP program, no one was willing to jeopardize their ability to raise precious funding. Every North Side school seemed to be competing for the same scarce resources, whether it was children, grants, or private donations. The parent leaders at successful public schools all seemed to fear that sharing fundraising information would only shrink the pie.

Fortunately, Ted found experts who were willing to help a little neighborhood school find its way. Unlike public schools, Chicago's most prestigious private schools hardly considered Nettelhorst a threat and were more than happy to share their expertise. From these conversations, Ted quickly surmised that raising money was indeed a very serious game, with fixed rules, strategies, winners, and losers. The school needed a comprehensive fundraising plan. Beyond silent auctions and paper flower sales, reformers needed to think bigger. Corporations, foundations, and even private donors were giving away millions of dollars each year to worthy causes.[5] If Nettelhorst didn't start playing the fundraising game with the big boys, development would never reach its full potential.

## ACCEPT A NEW PARADIGM

Ted also spoke to development experts at public and private universities in Chicago and throughout the country who insisted that Nettelhorst needed to understand the school's unique place in the funding world. First and foremost, Nettelhorst needed to get over the emotional hurdle that said it was elitist or impolitic for a neighborhood public school to raise funds, either externally or internally. Most private schools and many public schools across the country were raising millions of dollars each year from private donations. If Nettelhorst couldn't accept the fact that the school was becoming less attractive to funders each year and reframe its pitch accordingly, its financial situation was only going to get worse.

The experts insisted that Nettelhorst needed to come to terms with three sobering realities:

- One, it is a fact that money follows low-income children. When Nettelhorst stopped being a receiving school, it enrolled fewer students whose families lived below the poverty line. Although well over half the student population still qualified for free and reduced lunch, the school's student population was still more affluent than most other CPS schools. *Consequently, Nettelhorst would be a difficult choice for a donor angling to help disadvantaged students.*
- Two, it is a fact that money follows minority students. One unintended consequence from the board's decision to stop busing in stu-

dents from overcrowded schools was that Nettelhorst now enrolled fewer African American and Hispanic students. Even though the school boasted textbook multicultural diversity from preschool through eighth grade, with students and staff members conversing in over thirty different languages, it now had far more self-declared Caucasian students than most other public schools in Chicago.[6] *Consequently, Nettelhorst would be a difficult choice for a donor angling to help minority students.*

- And three, it is a fact that money follows underperforming students. Nettelhorst had the proud distinction of being named a CPS Rising Star school, one of the top twenty schools in Chicago for test score gains. Plus, Nettelhorst's new community school status made the school an unlikely candidate for any new über-educational pilot program that might command federal funds or state earmarks. *Consequently, Nettelhorst would be a difficult choice for a donor angling to help underperforming students or promote the next trend in educational solutions.*

For any entity that traditionally supported inner-city public school education, Nettelhorst had paradoxically become too much of everything: too smart, too rich, too white, too small, and even too average. The neighborhood might have turned its little ugly duckling into a swan, but from a development perspective, the school ran the risk of becoming less and less lovable every day.

In truth, Nettelhorst wasn't trapped in a financial no man's land. While the school seemed to have become a philanthropic pariah, it still had a few cards to play. Thanks to rising test scores, increased enrollment, and generous exposure, the greater school community had come to understand the symbiotic relationship between a quality neighborhood and a quality neighborhood public school. Reformers just needed to once again rewrite the Nettelhorst story to capitalize on what the school had become.

The bedrock of Nettelhorst's new development story would be an ambitious $230,000 parent-driven capital campaign to renovate the school's science lab and the auditorium. This plan would also test the group's ability to fundraise in a directed, considered, and focused manner. The team allocated $120,000 for its first big-ticket project, the renovation of the large auditorium, because its seating, sound, and lighting were broken or nonexistent. Nettelhorst was fortunate enough to have an auditorium that didn't double as a gym or a lunchroom, but for a school that professed to showcase the arts, it was a particularly troubling situation. Hopeful reformers had a renovation plan handoff ready, but neither private nor public funding ever materialized.[7] The team allocated $110,000 for the second project, the renovation of Nettelhorst's aging science lab, which suffered from broken equipment and an outdated curriculum. Beyond the science lab and auditorium renovations, the team also had a long-term goal of building an "opportunity fund" to provide reserves so that the school could quickly take advantage of matching grants and meet unforeseen budgetary needs (with an initial target of $50,000). Moreover, if every household is supposed to have a rainy day fund, reformers looked to the sky, and saw dark clouds on the horizon. An "opportunity fund" could just as easily become an "emergency fund" if Springfield's public school coffers suddenly ran dry.

## TARGET DEVELOPMENT AUDIENCES

Community members might be willing to support the school's desire to improve arts and science, but donors weren't going to fall from the sky. The school needed to understand its development audience in terms of concentric circles of interest: alumni, current and potential parents, community members, corporations, and foundations. The first challenge was to access the school's deep alumni base. Although Nettelhorst was one of Chicago's oldest, and at times most prestigious, elementary schools, the existing FON alumni lists were so jumbled and incomplete that they were virtually useless. Confidentiality issues further prevented CPS from releasing the limited contacts it did have on file. If the school had any hope of courting alumni (big donors or otherwise), a long road lay ahead. Supermom Lisa Levens, the team's point person in charge of alumni relations, had created a robust spreadsheet of alumni addresses, e-mail addresses, and phone numbers, but she warned that information on interests and giving histories might take years to build, if it could be accessed at all.

The school might see more immediate results if it reframed its relationship with the community in terms of long-term, recurrent giving. Reformers had already proved adept at soliciting in-kind donations, yet most contacts were quickly forged to help with an immediate need and dropped just as quickly when the project was completed. In fact, early reformers never managed to create a comprehensive donor list or resource book. Though it had been their intention, reformers did not even send thank you notes or tax exemption letters in a timely manner. Unfortunately, their incompetence often registered as ingratitude; initially enthusiastic professionals became hard to reach, tradesmen were reluctant to help more than once, and local business owners were still encouraging but tapped out. The new mindset wouldn't prevent reformers from continuing to source projects with urgent, oftentimes kooky, needs—disco balls, floor tile, tennis balls, as well as office furniture and books—but they did need to move beyond hit-and-run tactics. Nettelhorst mom Cheryl Simon brought the school's hobbled external communications up to private school standards, seemingly overnight.

One approach conceived within the new strategy was the innovative idea of the Nettelhorst Network, a program in which a business would agree to donate a portion of its proceeds to Nettelhorst in exchange for marketing in the monthly school newsletter and on its website. While a 20 percent donation might not seem like much return on a single waffle or cup of coffee, small change could add up quickly; when realtors offered the same percentage back on commissions from Nettelhorst referrals, the return could amount to thousands of dollars.

Again, this kind of networking scheme would only succeed if Nettelhorst could convince donors of three fundamental truths:

- One, Nettelhorst's families would present a legitimate and responsive market.

- Two, a donor's information would be effectively disseminated to parents in a credible manner.
- And three, the school would spend the investment wisely.

Merchants needed to see their relationship with Nettelhorst as a long-term and mutually beneficial investment.

## REFINE THE ASK

Perhaps the greater school community hadn't given to Nettelhorst in significant amounts because the school hadn't requested the donation properly. Just as early reformers developed a comprehensive story of renewal to entice neighborhood families, the fundraising team developed an overall concept to appeal to the new target audience. The reincarnated marketing scheme included posters and postcards, a media kit, an interactive website, a sophisticated presentation, and a charming fundraising thermometer posted on the school's exterior, asking passersby, "How much $$$ does it take to dream a giraffe?" The team's whole presentation said smart, professional, and cool.

Because a directed giving campaign would inspire more contributions—and contributions at higher levels—than the undirected "please give to the school" method, the team identified key projects and developed detailed proposals. The team's PowerPoint presentation to potential donors outlined *exactly* how people could become involved. It showed how the school would utilize donations with colorful charts, graphs, and line-by-line budgets to inspire confidence in the school's ability to steward investments. The presentation also helped place the school in historical context, both as a Chicago landmark and as an educational institution. Nettelhorst had become a viable neighborhood school that not only improved property values and quality of life, but one that would be a model for the city and nation. In the past, reformers had reached out to the community for support, but never managed to translate sympathy or inspiration into action. The new fundraising package, on the other hand, spelled out exactly what the school needed and exactly how individuals could help.

## DEVELOP A CULTURE OF ADVOCACY

Now that the team had a convincing sales pitch with a "hard close," Nettelhorst's parents and students needed to become integral, long-term financial supporters and advocates of the school. In the new scheme, Susan's beloved low-level fundraiser would still have a place in Nettelhorst's comprehensive fundraising plan, not only because it was profitable but because the activity created an army of child advocates. For example, a new member of the Nettelhorst Community Group (NCG) steering committee, Melanie Glick, initiated a monthly out-of-uniform day for the school, when students could dress in civilian clothes if they donated two dollars for a fund that would be used to purchase sports team uniforms and to provide school uniforms for needy families.[8] It seemed like a simple way for students to show their Nettelhorst spirit while raising money to support the school. And, just as she predicted, the new out-of-uniform day raised over a thousand dollars each month, like clockwork.

However, some parents from both ends of the economic spectrum found Melanie's new fundraising concept jarring. While the suggested donation of two dollars wasn't mandatory and all students could come to school out of uniform, some wondered why a public school was asking for money at all. Wasn't that why they paid taxes? Furthermore, even though students had been asked to bring donations in a sealed envelope, surely many would come to know whose envelopes were light and whose were heavy. While a couple of dollars might be the price of a double latte for some parents, others were struggling to come up with forty cents for the reduced-price school lunch. If the purpose of wearing a school uniform was to counteract class distinctions, wasn't this fundraiser unwittingly fostering inequality?

If the monthly out-of-uniform day was fermenting class conflict, the team needed to rethink the idea of fundraising competitions between grades or between classrooms. The team wondered why the national fundraising companies, who motivated child-peddlers with useless trinkets, didn't exacerbate socioeconomic tensions. When the team tried an inter-classroom competition with the Box Tops for Education fundraiser, competition didn't cause any problems; however, the activity didn't seem to create a school-wide spirit of philanthropy, either. The team needed a new approach that somehow reimagined the school's climate of care.

The team decided to try to change the culture of gift giving at the school. Nettelhorst asked parents and students to consider donating new books to the library in place of birthday presents or teacher appreciation gestures. The team created special bookplates to commemorate gifts and publically thanked children for their generosity in the school's newsletter. Whereas birthday donations to favorite charities might have read as forced altruism, donating library books seemed appropriate and child-driven. After all, every student could reap the rewards of the gift, including the birthday boy or girl. Teachers needed a well-stocked library far more than they needed another scented candle or coffee mug. The team fully expected that birthday children would still receive new bicycles and roller skates and teachers would continue to be rewarded as well, but perhaps the school could also inspire generosity by allowing students to see themselves as capable agents for positive change at the school.

## IDENTIFY POTENTIAL GIVERS

The team also encouraged parents to become personal advocates by soliciting family and friends directly—people were likely to make a charitable contribution to some organization, and it might as well be to Nettelhorst. The team gave every parent at the school a fundraising jump-start kit to help them become comfortable soliciting donations. The materials outlined Nettelhorst's goals and needs, and even offered talking points and specific catchphrases, such as, "If you donate to three good causes this year, I hope Nettelhorst, your (granddaughter's, nephew's, etc.) elementary school, is one of them." Parents merely needed to personalize a stock introductory letter and e-mail it on to friends and family. Parents didn't have to personally collect donations, either; the letter would direct the recipient to the school's new website, which included all the necessary information and allowed for online contributions. Parents didn't have to extend themselves beyond a simple, "Hello, thought you might be interested in little Jack or Jill's life . . ."

The team also asked parents to help identify major givers (in the $1,000-plus range) through family or work connections. Whereas universities and private schools were particularly skillful in aligning a major donor's background and interests with specific projects, Nettelhorst had a surplus of projects but did not have any big donor names from which to draw. The team asked parents to lead them to family or work connections for advice (not cash), hoping that any connection might help accelerate major-gift fundraising.

In what would have been unimaginable in the early days of the reform movement, parents themselves became major donors—one anonymous parent donated $30,000 to the school. While a parent who had the means to donate thousands of dollars was a rarity, if the team hadn't provided a framework for understanding how his donation would be used, this parent never would have had the confidence to give to Nettelhorst. And, of course, had the school not made a point of asking parents to help in the first place, there would have been no gift at all.

The team also asked parents to provide contacts from a prescreened list of targeted corporations and foundations, knowing that any introduction at all could help turn a cold lead into a warm one. Parents did not even have to reach out to their contacts themselves. All they needed to do was provide the contact information, including a short note on the nature of the relationship and any other pertinent details, and the team's semitrained "relationship managers" would handle the rest. Parents did not need to worry that the relationship managers would muck up their personal or professional contacts; the managers were not calling to ask for money, but were merely asking to gain a personal introduction within the company.

If parents seemed reluctant to provide their contacts, the team encouraged them to remember that philanthropic organizations exist solely to partner with groups that match their criteria. The team had already prescreened each organization and determined it to be an appropriate match by scouring Donors Forum. Nettelhorst was as much of an opportunity for the organization as the organization was for Nettelhorst. While parents were doing the school a favor by turning over their personal contacts, *Nettelhorst was really doing a favor for them.*

Within a matter of months, the team had its first big score with a $50,000 gift from the L&R Anixter Foundation to renovate the science lab. The story of that donation unfolded in exactly the remarkable—yet unremarkable—way Ted's contacts had suggested the philanthropic world worked. The initial contact with Anixter came about because a Nettelhorst parent was talking about public schools with a coworker and the conversation turned toward Nettelhorst and fundraising. As it happened, the associate served on the board of a major family foundation; the parent invited the associate to visit the school and meet with the principal. The thrilled associate returned from his visit to Nettelhorst, bubbling with all the amazing things that were going on at this little public school, so members of the foundation decided to visit the school themselves. After having a sandwich across the street at the Melrose Diner, the associate returned with a promise to help out with the science lab renovation.

Steve Anixter explained why he felt comfortable donating to Nettelhorst: "We were impressed the moment we walked into the school . . . Lots of warmth and a lot of feeling that there were many components at work to enrich the kids' lives. We found a very dedicated group of teachers, and equally dedicated parents seeing that their kids are getting the best education possible. The way they've done it is to put in the time and effort to make it all happen."

Obviously, Steve Anixter never would have chosen to donate to Nettelhorst if the school seemed an unworthy or incapable steward of the investment. But what got the ball rolling was a parent simply talking enthusiastically about her neighborhood school. Similar conversations proved just as powerful. As parents talked about the school's new science directive, a contact at a major pharmaceutical company showed interest; the contact's school visit resulted in a new science curriculum for the school. Reformers were awestruck to find that, with a little luck and perseverance, seemingly minor conversations could snowball into major gifts.

One might argue that only a privileged population has these kinds of chance encounters. In this case, it was not so much *who* was having the conversation, but the fact that it was taking place at all. Nettelhorst parents had the school on their minds day and night and would talk about the reform movement to anyone within earshot. Just as the infrastructure team had asked parents to keep Nettelhorst in mind as they window-shopped and the marketing team had asked parents to talk up the school in the parks, the fundraising team asked parents to keep the question "What can you do for my school?" on an endlessly running loop. If parents could learn to keep their eyes and ears open, the law of six degrees of separation could play out in any chance encounter on a bus or a plane, at work, in the gym, or at the supermarket. Amazingly, parents from across the economic spectrum sparked major donations because they learned to insert Nettelhorst into their personal dialogue. If anyone showed the slightest interest, the school had a sophisticated plan in place to facilitate any level of giving, rather than just an overturned, empty hat.

Just as the infrastructure team found that it needed an advocate to access any kind of corporate donation, the fundraising team always looked to anyone on the inside who might champion Nettelhorst's cause. When parents discovered a potential lead, the team asked everyone to help flush out a contact. For example, if the news of a new Widget Corporation initiative surfaced, the team would send out e-mails to parents to deliver *any* contact within the Widget Corporation. The team even went so far as to give parents a sample script to personalize:

> Hi! Hope everything is going well with you! I wanted to ask if you knew anyone at the Widget Corporation; we've put together a pretty deep plan for overhauling the science labs and curriculum at our school, and the Widget Corporation announced that they're going to

fund such initiatives (I've pasted the article below). I'd love to meet with them and show them what we're up to, but none of our parents know anyone there. If you have a contact, or could lead me to one, I'd appreciate it. Our plans are right in line with theirs. If you have time, I'd love to show you the progress we've made . . .

After a long chain of e-mails bouncing to different people through cyberspace, lo and behold, someone would actually discover a contact at the Widget Corporation! The friend-of-a-friend-of-a-friend would e-mail the Widget Corporation contact and copy back to Ted:

> By way of this e-mail, I wanted to introduce you to Ted, who is an excellent fundraiser for Nettelhorst School. He sent me the e-mail and article below about your amazing plans. I have a friend who has children attending that school (she loves it!). Could you put them in touch with whoever is leading the school aspect of this initiative? I know you have a million other priorities, but this would be a benefit to the Widget Company, too, because this school is one of the best stories in the city. You are both copied on this e-mail so you guys can connect directly. Let me know if you have any questions!

While this sliver of an introduction would hardly guarantee that Nettelhorst would win the Widget Corporation grant, it just might help facilitate the initial relationship. As the team explored potential relationships, anything that might turn a cold lead into a warm prospect was fair game. As every salesperson knows, more calls mean more sales. If it took ten calls to close a deal, the team knew that it might have to make the *other* nine calls before it could celebrate a victory.

The drive to gain a personal introduction might appear unseemly, but if this is the way the philanthropy world works, why should only a select few schools (mostly private, in any case) know how to play the game? Again, unlike underperforming or underprivileged schools, an underfunded middle-class school is more or less on its own to shore up the state funding gap. It is understandable if few people become misty-eyed: A school located in a middle-class neighborhood has greater potential for investment and capable money management than a similar school located in an underprivileged neighborhood. However, it would be overly simplistic to assume that a middle-class neighborhood will readily invest in its neighborhood public school with capital any more than it will magically invest with its own children.

To be sure, Nettelhorst was extremely fortunate. The school was lucky to have a select group of parents who had the energy and wherewithal to host fundraisers, write grant proposals, and create presentations. For all its hard work, the team showed remarkable early progress. CPS began to link Nettelhorst's website to its own site to show how schools might set up their own fundraising effort. At Nettelhorst's second silent/live auction, planners knocked it out of the park, tripling the previous year's attendance and netting $65,000 for the school. In less than a year, the fundraising team's capital campaign to renovate the science lab and the auditorium raised over $200,000 from private and corporate donors.

The development team also learned to read the waters. In the past, when the school identified an immediate need, parents looked to individuals to help satisfy those needs in piecemeal fashion. In the new world order, the team had prepared scores of proposals that addressed issues from across the educational spectrum. If and when the fundraising team identified a potential "live" donor, it worked from the donor's interests, backward. Case in point: In what promises to become a deep and mutually beneficial long-term relationship, the Blackhawks, Chicago's professional hockey team, donated $210,000 to help launch the school's sports, health, and wellness initiative. This partnership only came about because the development team anticipated the donor's needs with a handoff-ready proposal. Again, the Blackhawks never would have signed on unless they had believed that Nettelhorst would steward their investment. To be sure, generating numerous, professional-quality proposals is difficult and time-consuming. But in today's economic climate, a school fundraising team with an empty briefcase works with a clear disadvantage.

Beyond skill and luck, Nettelhorst's development team also had moxie. When a local paper announced that a museum planned to donate a ton of cash to deserving public schools, the team promptly called the museum's community outreach officer and asked for a meeting. As it turned out, the reporter got the story wrong. Ted said, "Wow, I guess your phone has been ringing off the hook." "No, actually," he responded, "you're the only school that called."

Which begs the question: Why was Nettelhorst the only school to pick up the phone and call the museum? When the Blackhawks were shopping for a public school to invest in, why was Nettelhorst the only school that offered them a handoff-ready game plan? Why aren't more public schools out there hustling?

Part of the answer lies in the fact that most schools, even very successful ones, do not understand that the funding game has changed—or if they do, they lack the means to play competitively. Nettelhorst reformers, for all their incredible energy and talent, waited four years before the school could even approach fundraising in any meaningful way. The roadblocks were confounding: Until the neighborhood invested in the school with its energy, and most importantly with its children, extra funding would have likely fallen into a black hole. When the school radically changed the educational paradigm and became worthy of investment, it was exceedingly fortunate to have the human capital to confront the funding crisis head-on. In the new world order, Nettelhorst still had a place for two-dollar paper tulip fundraisers, but the school also yearned to reach a little higher.

Without a doubt, it is a sad state of affairs that individual schools must devote so much effort to raising private funds for public education. Critics might question whether parents would be better served putting their limited energy into political lobbying than amassing gift baskets for a silent auction or scouring corporate donor lists.

Surely schools would have more power if they pooled their energy and lobbied the state legislature for more funding overall. A great model for such a concerted effort is A+ Illinois, a broad-based advocacy group committed to improving the way in which Illinois funds and supports public education.

While the full answer to this call to action is rarely spoken in public and some members on the fundraising team applauded A+ Illinois's lobbying efforts, they suspected that Nettelhorst would be better served if the team directed its limited energy to trying to help the school, rather than trying to help every school in the state. As evidence, they pointed to A+ Illinois' "billion-dollar bake sale" in 2007, when school children, parents, and reporters arrived at the capitol rotunda to remind Illinois legislators about the urgent need to improve school funding. From all corners, A+ Illinois deemed the protest a resounding success.

However, at the end of the legislative session, lawmakers didn't go in for the $2 billion cookie to increase the state's shamelessly low per-pupil spending; or the $498 million brownie to fund special education; or the $500 million cupcake for capital improvements; or the $370 million pie for preschool and early childhood programs; or the $306 million doughnut for underperforming schools; or the $196 million muffin to expand full-day kindergarten; or even the $78 million slice of banana bread to provide training and incentives for teachers, principals, and administrators.[9]

Unfortunately, the current funding chasm has become so deep and so wide that political activism might not make much of a dent. Pretend that the Illinois legislature decided to allocate more revenue toward public education, raising the state's deplorable ranking from forty-ninth to, say, forty-eighth or even thirty-eighth in the country—what then? Yes, every penny counts, but how much of an increase would that improvement really generate for each individual school when spread across the entire state? Unless the political climate for funding public education changes dramatically, parents and principals must learn to help themselves.

However, in the midst of this final lesson on school fundraising, it is important to keep in mind two key points. One, extra funding is meaningless if a school cannot spend it wisely. And two, the school's climate of care was, in fact, the only thing that really mattered. Money did not power the Nettelhorst revolution. People did.

# SEVEN

# THE NETTELHORST
# BLUEPRINT

W HEN THE Roscoe Park Eight banded together to embrace their local school, they enlisted new recruits with the parting salvo, "Welcome to our little revolution." Their idea *was* revolutionary; the notion that parents could simply walk in from off the street and fix a broken public elementary school was the stuff of urban myth. These moms-turned-reformers harbored no lofty ambitions to reform public education in any systemic way. Rather, they needed to upgrade only one school—Nettelhorst Elementary—so that their children could be assured of enrollment in a quality institution. If they failed to turn around their neighborhood school within a matter of months, each family would be compelled to pay for private school, take its chances in the public school lottery, or move to the suburbs. In a curious mix of energy, hubris, and naiveté, the young women viewed fixing Nettelhorst as the path of least resistance.

## FROM DREAMS TO REALITY

As the women schemed and plotted in the local diner, they were too green to know that one generally measures school reform in decades, not months. Even though Nettelhorst had pulled out of its twenty-year nosedive, the school still needed dramatic improvement before neighborhood parents would be willing to enroll their children. While early reformers may have doubted that Nettelhorst would uphold its end of the bargain, Susan had every confidence that her school would deliver. She issued a challenge: If the park parents could round up just twenty neighborhood children, she promised that her rickety plane would give them all safe passage to eighth grade.

This test appeared simultaneously facile and implausible; how could they convince twenty families to gamble with their children's education when Nettelhorst lacked desirable test scores, a welcoming infrastructure, or even a decent reputation? Virtually everyone in the community had written off the school as a lost cause. As the reformers advocated for their cause at their little city playground, they had no way of knowing that there were hundreds of parents with young children in other nearby parks, all just as desperate for guaranteed admission to a quality public school and also willing to work for it.

Within the span of five years, the reformers' grassroots movement created a school that was not only viable, but became one of Chicago's most progressive and desirable institutions. Today, prospective parents pack the weekly story time and parent-led tours. The school has become so popular that Nettelhorst's Preschool for All and TBP programs boast deep waiting lists. So many neighborhood parents elect to stay on for kindergarten that Nettelhorst rarely accepts students from outside the district for any grade, including preschool. Parents volunteer in almost every classroom. Teachers can be found in their classrooms until late in the evening and they come back in on weekends. Nettelhorst's innovative fee-for-service community school has become a national model, awarded the Dimon Distinguished Community Schools Award as one of the top ten community schools in Illinois. Neighborhood children fill the playgrounds after school and on weekends. The energy in the school is palpable.

The school's vibrant environment continues to evolve and inspire. Public spaces aren't static stage sets but ever-changing tableaus. For example, when the school received a large donation of outdoor cushions, the world music cafe for upper-grade students morphed into a Middle

Eastern media lounge. The Atlantis hallway has inspired a new underwater kickball game. The glitter tree has inspired a game in which kids chase the reflective dots like fireflies. The community kitchen feels more homely every day.

Beyond making occupants happy, the school's infrastructure improvements have helped to facilitate additional parent-led reforms. When the Nettelhorst Community Group (NCG) showcased a major sports, health, and wellness initiative to the Blackhawks, the renovated playgrounds, community kitchen, compost bins, recycled art, and music-filled lunchroom helped make a convincing argument that the school community was serious about nutrition, cooking, health, and fitness. The Nettelhorst movement bucks the conventional wisdom that says that school environments only change after the culture changes. Reformers found that by changing the school environment first, the school's culture improved dramatically.

Nettelhorst's community of care has become a powerful force. For example, when a Nettelhorst parent was diagnosed with cancer, she found the outpouring of support from the school community overwhelming. The NCG organized nightly take-home dinners for her family for over a year. "Lucky doesn't describe it," the mom confided. "It feels like it must have been decades ago when people took the time to care for their friends. My husband and I look back at some choices we made over the years and realize how this school has become so much more to us than a great place for my daughter to get an education. Where else in a big city like Chicago is there a more robust network of people who have common goals that have become so much of a family? What a rare opportunity." Over and again, parents cite Nettelhorst's great community as one of the school's most defining features.

Nettelhorst also delivered on academics: CPS named Nettelhorst a Rising Star school, as one of the top twenty schools in Chicago for academic gains. In five years, ISAT test scores more than tripled. Neighborhood parents held on tight during the turbulence early on, and were rewarded when many of the school's testing problems solved themselves.

In fact, when the first group of neighborhood children in TBP reached third grade, their tests were scored at 100 percent in math and 91 percent in reading, among the highest scores in the city.

Reform measures did indeed benefit all of Nettelhorst's population, not just the newly enrolled neighborhood families. In 2007, over half, and in 2008, *all* of the graduating eighth-graders (75 percent of whom lived below the poverty level) scored high enough on the ISAT exam to attend the CPS selective high school of their choosing. One graduating student received a full scholarship to attend *any* private school in the United States. The Roscoe Park Eight may have focused on the younger grades, but Susan made sure that their self-interest worked to everyone's benefit.

Since academic performance is closely tied to family income, critics might argue that the sharp rise in test scores can be attributed to Nettelhorst's changing demographics more than any other factor. While the board did stop busing in students from overcrowded schools, almost all of Nettelhorst's bused-in students chose to remain at the school until they graduated. While the influx of middle-class families did lower Nettelhorst's overall poverty rate, in 2007, 40 percent of Nettelhorst students still came from families who lived below the poverty line. The natural attrition of bused-in students might explain a gradual improvement in test scores over time, but Nettelhorst's scores rose sharply across every grade, almost immediately.

Since academic performance is also linked to race, critics might also argue that Nettelhorst's rising scores are the natural result of replacing minority children with Caucasian children. Despite the influx of neighborhood children, Nettelhorst actually became *more* racially diverse, not less. In 2007, the school's racial demographics broke down to approximately 25 percent African American, 25 percent Hispanic, 40 percent Caucasian, and 10 percent Asian. Many students do not speak English as their primary language at home.[1] Again, the natural attrition of predominately African American and Hispanic bused-in students might explain a gradual shift but can't account for the sudden rise in test scores for either the school's bused-in minority students or for the incoming neighborhood children.

If race or income weren't the driving forces, how could one explain the school's dramatic about-face? Although the school's demographics changed over time, Susan's guiding principals did not. Reformers did not expect her to be anything other than a first-rate educator. She didn't need to be a crackerjack expert in fundraising, marketing, public relations, decorating, party planning, or community organizing. Susan had the confidence to admit that she wasn't an expert in any of these areas and was willing to trust community members who were experts. In exchange for their free advice and volunteer labor, reformers expected her to run a school and run it well. Parents were confident that she shared their vision for school improvement, which included small classes, high-caliber teaching, professional development, and expanded enrichment opportunities. Reformers had faith that the school would deliver on all these fronts—and it did, in spades.

With the school free to focus on raising the academic bar, reformers could mobilize local resources to improve other aspects of school, which in turn enriched the entire community. Nettelhorst did not exist within a vacuum. If the school had any hope of reaching its full potential, it needed the support of the greater school community. The school needed a more salient message to entice the entire community to give the neighborhood's ugly duckling a second look.

A "new and improved" Nettelhorst became part of the neighborhood milieu, seemingly overnight. For example, when the farmers' market was preparing to open for its second year, a stranger picked up a Nettelhorst French Market postcard at the coffee shop, turned to Jacqueline in line, and said, "Oh, look, that adorable farmers' market is starting again at the school—I look forward to that every year!" In only one season, the Nettelhorst French Market, a mixed-use concept that had initially so flummoxed city planners and CPS property managers, had become a highly anticipated annual rite. Just as quickly, neighborhood families began to expect that the local chamber of commerce would always host elaborate parties at the school, like the Halloween Hoopla and the Little Bunny Egg Hunt. The neighborhood even came to count on the school's public art happenings, such as the students tying colorful fabric "intentions" to the fence at the end of the year, as if these traditions had always existed. In part due to Nettelhorst's revival, East Lakeview has become one of Chicago's most desirable neighborhoods.[2]

## MY SANDBOX, YOUR SANDBOX

Critics witnessing Nettelhorst's success might argue that its reformation was possible because of a happy confluence of three unique social forces, and consequently, would be a difficult model to replicate. First, Nettelhorst's neighborhood presented an exceptionally hospitable environment. Over twenty years ago, the gay community and die-hard leftists gentrified the East Lakeview/Boystown neighborhood. The neighborhood matured into a racially and socioeconomically diverse area that seemed to tolerate everyone. Critics might argue that the neighborhood was hardly accepting of the school's bused-in population and only embraced Nettelhorst as a whole *after* the school's more unruly students became less visible. Critics might further argue that it is hardly a feat that sprightly young mothers could galvanize resources in a welcoming neighborhood full of idealists, activists, and affluence.

Second, naysayers might question whether the Roscoe Park Eight were really typical of prospective public school parents at all. Who were these liberal elitists with their wooden toys, fancy strollers, and endless leisure time to volunteer for lost causes? How realistic is it to find educated, skilled professionals splitting their attention between making sand castles with their toddlers and organizing a grassroots school reform?

And third, critics might question just how many public school principals are willing to let neighborhood parents (whose kids don't even go to their school) come in and see their school, warts and all? Susan made for somewhat of a renegade: Nearing the end of her career, she never worried about losing her job or her pension, and she often took a Mae West, "Let them fire me," approach to the board. Because she shared a similar cultural background to the Roscoe Park Eight, she was unthreatened and unthreatening. How realistic is it that a principal who is less cavalier, less experienced, or less culturally aligned to neighborhood families would be able to replicate the Nettelhorst model?

In answer to these questions, it is safe to say that the Roscoe Park Eight were indeed an extraordinary group of women, living in an extraordinary neighborhood, with the good fortune of finding an extraordinary principal. However, in many ways, Nettelhorst's zeitgeist was hardly unique. The logistical benefits of East Lakeview surely played a role: The school sat squarely in the middle of a densely populated urban setting, in close proximity to parks and public transportation; numerous restaurants and coffeehouses facilitated impromptu meetings and chance encounters. Plus, the school's proximity to Boystown, Chicago's vibrant gay community, delivered a seemingly endless supply of creative talent to Nettelhorst's front door. Yet Chicago is divided into sixteenths, with each segment served by a neighborhood school—the creativity, resources, and energy of East Lakeview's tiny parcel are refracted hundreds of times over in neighborhoods throughout the city.

In terms of leadership, Susan was a dynamic educator, but she was not a perfect administrator. Indeed, most urban public school principals face the same complex staff issues, budget limitations, and environmental stressors she did. A great many public school principals also share her expertise, passion, and commitment to educating children, and many would be willing to partner with neighborhood parents if they could only envision the product they could build together.

While East Lakeview is a great neighborhood, Chicago is a city of great neighborhoods. During the nineties, Chicago, like many cities across the country, began to remake itself, renovating run-down areas and enticing middle-class families to immigrate back to the city. Low-income neighborhoods with few amenities became bustling middle- to upper-middle-class areas filled with diverse markets, retail areas, restaurants, and entertainment venues. A great many middle-class parents, who are rarely speculative urban pioneers, would love to remain in their neighborhoods if they could only solve the elementary school dilemma.

The moms and dads around the Roscoe Park sandbox were talented, to be sure, but they are representative of a typical segment of Chicago's middle-class parent base. As couples wait until later in life to begin their families, it becomes more the norm to find a mom or dad who has made a conscious decision to put a lucrative career on hold to parent full-time. In Chicago, as in many cities, the mothers and fathers wiping noses and changing diapers likely hold advanced degrees and impressive résumés; they welcome the opportunity to apply their skills in a new direction, especially for the benefit of their children. And again, a successful reform movement requires only a handful of really dedicated, skilled leaders. To the talented parents who doubt they have the energy or time to work on a neighborhood school in transition, there's truth to the old saw that many hands make light work. Many Nettelhorst reformers were exceedingly fortunate to have a support structure at home that allowed them the freedom to work on the fly or sneak away to their clandestine meetings at the diner. As more and more families embrace shared parenting, household chores, and flexible work schedules, grassroots reform movements are ever more likely to succeed.

The Roscoe Park Eight certainly had an advantage because they genuinely enjoyed each other's company, and many park parents signed on as a way to bond with their peers. The stroller-parent community can be shockingly familiar and intimate, yet at the same time, alienating and trivial. The desire for connection and meaning is hardly unique to an East Lakeview playlot.

Reformers were lucky to have respected community members advise them along the way. In particular, Marilyn Eisenberg, the visionary leader of the 1970s Nettelhorst reform movement, offered tons of guidance and encouragement. However, the Roscoe Park sandbox, like all sandboxes, did not exist within a vacuum. If schools can articulate a clear and compelling problem to solve, many community elders, experts, and movers and shakers will no doubt emerge to lend their expertise.

Neighborhood reformers faced many challenges that were hardly unique. Like most parents with young children, co-op parents had little energy to exert beyond what might further their families' immediate self-interest. However altruistic park parents imagined themselves to be, everyone complained that they didn't have the time or energy to assume parental responsibilities for children who seemed to be unsupported. For instance, when Susan insisted that co-op parents support the eighth-grade car wash to raise money for the class graduation party, she did not mean for co-op parents to simply drive to the school to have their cars washed. Rather, they were expected to arrive at the car wash by seven in the morning to wash cars alongside the eighth-graders, and to remain there *all day*. This was no laughing matter, as shirking child care for an entire Saturday meant paying a sitter or bribing a spouse. Reformers were incensed to discover that they were, in fact, the *only* parents in attendance, and left the day exhausted and deflated, feeling unappreciated by the eighth-grade students and their teachers. While Susan hoped that the neighborhood parents would come to regard *all* the school's children as their personal responsibility, sleep-deprived reformers, already stretched thin while juggling the demands of Nettelhorst, career, and family, simply didn't have the energy to be every kid's parent.

Beyond disparities between the treatment of the upper and lower grades, reformers quickly learned that they needed to become more attuned to disparities among families of children in the lower grades. Whereas most incoming neighborhood parents thought the heavily subsidized TBP was a bargain compared to what they would pay for a private preschool or a full-time nanny, many of Nettelhorst's current TBP parents struggled to pay the $185 weekly tuition. Many of the parents found the TBP tuition prohibitive, opting instead to enroll their children in the school's free state pre-K program (now called Preschool for All) that targeted "at-risk" children (as indicated by economic disadvantage, premature birth, or single-parent or foreign language households). Many state pre-K parents struggled to balance work commitments and preschool without the benefit of the TBP program's wraparound day care. If the movement couldn't bridge the gaps between the incoming preschool populations, socioeconomic disparities could become a tinderbox for unrest.

Just as Susan cautioned, every nuance of parent-driven school events held loaded messages to different populations—from the invitation, to the venue, to the kind of food served, to the scheduled date and time, to whether children were welcome at the event or if the school would provide on-site babysitting, to whether there would be a charge or a requested donation. After a few missteps, some key principles about social leveling emerged: All events held outside the school, even if free of charge, could potentially alienate some parents. Although the school as a venue held many drawbacks—partygoers couldn't drink, smoke, or easily park—it still proved a much safer choice than asking families to go to other locations. All social events needed to include children or offer free babysitting. Dads, who were traditionally marginalized by parent groups, would participate if they had their own father/child events.

## GROWING PAINS

As reformers began to enroll their own children in the school, Susan insisted that the Co-op needed to become more transparent and egalitarian. Whatever its initial successes were, the Co-op simply couldn't soldier on as an exclusive cabal, without any formalized structure or purpose. The Co-op had posted invitations to open meetings on the school doors and printed fliers for every student in both English and Spanish, but few Nettelhorst parents ever came. The consistently low turnout frustrated Susan—reformers simply weren't working hard enough to attract the parents.

The team captains countered that they didn't need crowded meetings; they needed meetings crowded with heavy lifters. The team captains were working overtime to market a "new and improved" Nettelhorst to neighborhood parents; if current Nettelhorst parents didn't already see the value of helping their child's school, reformers didn't have the time or energy to motivate them. The Roscoe Park Eight weren't interested in running a PTA; they were orchestrating a movement.

Even though reformers were in no mood to go on a fishing expedition for untapped talent, Susan felt certain that capable Nettelhorst parents would materialize if they only searched for them. Working parents might be skipping monthly meetings because of when they were scheduled, so the Co-op needed to offer every monthly co-op meeting *twice*, once after morning drop-off, and *again* in the evening. When Susan demanded to know how many people came to both the morning and evening co-op meetings, it became a running joke to report that the same cast of characters met after morning drop-off, then met again in the early evening, and then traded e-mails until three in the morning. But Susan wasn't laughing.

While Nettelhorst's current parents might not have seemed to be motivated, strategic thinkers, their participation was essential if reformers harbored any hopes to grow the movement beyond its start-up phase. Reformers needed to face facts: Nettelhorst's next principal (or even Susan, if the Co-op didn't deliver) could easily disband the Co-op if it didn't have a formalized structure or clear purpose. The Co-op needed to start looking and feeling like a regular PTA, with elections, agendas, bylaws, and mission statements; otherwise, the organization would not last.

To the core reformers, it seemed ridiculous to stray from the original team concept around which they had structured their work. The Co-op's mission was simple—everything needed to be done by anybody who wanted to help. Immediately. People needed to grab an oar—or at least have the courtesy to sit down in the boat. Park parents were rowing so furiously that any charge of elitism or cliquishness was just background static. To the outside world, the Roscoe Park Eight had become local superheroes. Somehow, someway, a band of neighborhood moms had managed to miraculously shock Nettelhorst back to life. If the school's internal critics couldn't appreciate what neighborhood parents brought to the school, a bunch of PTA or MBA rhetoric wouldn't help them see the big picture.

The Co-op needed to somehow transition leadership to a few of the many parents who at one time pledged their help to the Co-op, but do so without derailing the movement. Jacqueline never intended to become the group's poster child, but she had. On the one hand, the job came by default; most of the original reformers had moved away, left for private school, or had children who were still too young to attend the school. On the other hand, she embraced a role that counteracted the isolation and tedium of full-time childrearing. Although she got along well with the park regulars, she found the daily banter and gossip somewhat alienating; the Nettelhorst project acted as both social lubricant and emotional crutch. Like many a professional-turned-stay-at-home-mom, she found her new role left her desperate for validation, camaraderie, structure, and intellectual stimulation. While she adored her children and never regretted her choice to stay home full-time, spearheading the Nettelhorst movement offered a welcome sense of purpose and accomplishment.

However, Jacqueline quickly discovered that the role of Nettelhorst cheerleader had become a full-time job devoid of the formal trappings or benefits of paid employment or traditional volunteerism. She had temporarily left academia to take care of her family, but all the multitasking and stress of her new role were affecting her kids and straining her marriage; her incessant Nettelhorst scheming had long since worn out its welcome with her friends and acquaintances, and she feared that her relentless proselytizing had transformed her into one of East Lakeview's resident whack jobs. And yet, despite all the negatives, the challenge of fixing Nettelhorst had become something of a calling.

While Jacqueline's charisma and leadership energized the reform movement, her strong personality and unorthodox role made her an easy target within the school. The staff wondered why many questions about Nettelhorst from the outside world reached her ears before the principal's (understandable, given that the school's phones often went unanswered). If Jacqueline was supposed to be the Co-op's so-called media spokesperson, why did she seem to be speaking for the school so often? While sharing power might be essential to sound leadership, the limitless access and constant presence of Susan's sidekick were becoming a lightning rod for internal resentment and undermining Susan's authority. Nothing was to be gained if Nettelhorst's principal looked like a puppet. Despite the mutual respect and affection she shared with Jacqueline,

Susan was convinced that the reform movement would collapse if its cofounder could not, or would not, step aside.

By the summer of the second year, Jacqueline finally tired of all of the browbeating about "thoughtful succession," and without even consulting her compatriots, turned the Co-op's leadership over to a new Nettelhorst mom who seemed capable and enthusiastic. The move seemed impulsive but reasonable: Nettelhorst seemed to have finally hit its stride, many of the Roscoe Park Eight had moved on to other schools or other cities, and Jacqueline had scant interest in running an elementary school PTA. The Nettelhorst project proved to be a good life chapter, but now that both her children were in school all day, it seemed like a good time to return to a paying gig. She hoped that a fresh face for the Co-op would silence critics, and she could continue to quietly wield influence from behind the scenes.

Jacqueline's poor judgment almost led to the destruction of the Co-op. The new leader quickly discovered that reformers were far less enlightened in private than they seemed in public. Reformers were not the touchy-feely, optimistic love bugs she met on the tour or on the playground, but hard-nosed pragmatists who had little sympathy for anything or anyone that stood in their way. In her opinion, the clearest remedy was to disband the Co-op entirely and start a proper PTA. Fortunately, the mom became so disgusted with the uncensored Co-op that she unenrolled her child before school began and the mutiny could take hold. Having learned her lesson, Jacqueline vowed that she would not imperil the movement again; when the Co-op was on firmer ground, its next successor would be chosen carefully from within.

In the third year of the movement, Laura Holmes and Jane Cornett, two dedicated co-op moms, volunteered to colead the group. Jane managed a bookstore and Laura was finishing a degree in early education. Together, they formed the perfect team.[3] Using a gentle hand, Laura managed to recruit Nettelhorst's Hispanic and Asian community into the Co-op through her work teaching a free English as a Second Language (ESL) class at the school after drop-off. Jane miraculously transformed all the notes hastily written on cocktail napkins and random notebooks into a codified playbook, giving the Co-op some much-needed structure. Under their leadership, the Co-op became something that did indeed look and feel like a traditional PTA.

Which begs the question: If the Co-op desperately needed structure and legitimacy, why didn't reformers just start a PTA? Part of the reason why the Roscoe Park Eight shied away from a national organization had to do with the unique circumstances of how the mothers arrived at Nettelhorst's door in the first place. For more than twenty years, Nettelhorst hadn't established a PTA, and almost all parent involvement to that point had been negative. The "T" in PTA stands for teacher, and internal politics dominated Nettelhorst's teaching climate. As much as Susan wanted to entice current Nettelhorst parents to attend co-op meetings, reformers feared that a formal PTA might give the school's negative factions something concrete to rally against.

Under the Co-op's ragtag banner, reformers could carry on as they saw fit, unconstrained by a national charter. A PTA might very well open Pandora's box: How could neighborhood parents join a school's PTA if they didn't have children in attendance? What if the national PTA didn't think that reformers should be deliberating on internal hiring decisions? What if it didn't think that reformers should be out on their own talking to local politicians, the school board, or the media? What if it didn't think sexuality belonged under the public school diversity banner, or didn't find the neighborhood's ROTC drill practice in the playlot so whimsical? Even if a national organization was willing to let parents march to their own drumbeat, the marketing team had gone to great pains to brand the Co-op as some kind of "new and improved" parents' organization. The Co-op figured that an annual PTA membership plus dues would cost as much as printing fifteen-thousand full-color glossy postcards for the revolution: core reformers weighed all the pluses and minuses of joining a national organization, and opted to print postcards instead.

By the fifth year, the Co-op felt confident enough to radically restructure itself, voluntarily. With successive waves of talented parents coming in and the school on surer footing, the Co-op saw the value of combining with the school's fundraising arm, Friends of Nettelhorst, to become Nettelhorst Community Group (NCG). The new streamlined NCG helped the school decrease overlapping purposes, improve fundraising, recruit new volunteers, and facilitate internal and external communication. Five trusted and capable parents emerged to lead the NCG— Rachel Gross, Carol Collier, Stephanie Schrodt, Jennifer Howell, and Melanie Glick— all wonder women with considerable corporate management experience behind them. With the internal management of the Co-op finally under control, Jacqueline could focus on what she enjoyed: recruitment, media relations, artwork, and of course, her family. While the NCG structure became more formalized, the new-and-improved co-op group did not feel radically different from its early park days. Despite all its travails, the Co-op transformed into an inclusive and transparent organization, but on its own time and in its own way.

Neighborhood parents stumbled many times as their reform movement traveled from Roscoe Park to the Melrose Diner to the school. Contrary to accepted wisdom, school reform built on consensus is foolish when a school is under siege. Until Nettelhorst could neutralize its negative factions, only trusted stakeholders could hold a trusted seat at the table. Park parents had the freedom to run with innovative ideas, but Susan always held them accountable. Their grassroots organization evolved into a formalized structure, but it did so organically. Self-interest inspired community members to revitalize Nettelhorst, but ultimately, the school's climate of care is what convinced them to stay.

## REFORM IS A JOURNEY

While in many ways Nettelhorst is representative of many neighborhood public schools, the reformers were not oblivious to the fact that many factors worked in the school's favor. Nettelhorst was exceedingly fortunate to have so many stars in alignment. Obviously, the Nettelhorst blueprint is not wholly appropriate for every neighborhood. While every school and every neighborhood face barriers to student leaning and community involvement, underprivileged neighborhoods present significant challenges. Reformers cannot solicit donations from neighborhood merchants if neighborhood commerce doesn't exist; community members cannot volunteer if they struggle to meet basic personal needs; and a fee-for-service community school cannot survive without a paying client base. And, of course, the threat of violence curbs all participation: Children cannot play on a playground after school if they fear violence, any more than they can learn if their classrooms are under siege.

However, a key advantage of the traditional community school model is that it isn't one-size-fits-all. Every school can chart its own course given its unique set of stakeholders, needs, and challenges. Regardless of where a school finds itself on its journey, many of Nettelhorst's solutions may prove instructive.

Case in point: Just three years ago, Waters Elementary, in Chicago's gentrifying Ravenswood neighborhood was remarkably similar to Nettelhorst. Following the Nettelhorst blueprint, Terri Versace, Ravenswood's version of Jacqueline, organized neighborhood parents into a group called Waters Today.[4] Under Terri's leadership and with the help of the principal and current parents, enthusiastic neighborhood parents rolled up their sleeves and got to work. The group solicited in-kind donations to improve the school's infrastructure, devised better extracurricular offerings with newfound cultural partners, held parent-led tours and open houses, developed a comprehensive and creative marketing plan, and worked with the principal to bring in a TBP program, summer camps, and more extensive before- and after-school offerings. In just three years, enrollment more than doubled, and Waters is well on its way to becoming a school of choice for the neighborhood's middle-class families.

## A RISK OF FAITH

The success of the Nettelhorst reform movement was not certain. The school overcame many obstacles: Susan contended with naysayers, obstructionists, saboteurs, and sloths; reformers faced roadblocks, missteps, self-doubts, euphoric highs, and soul-crushing lows. The path to reform was not always easy, but the goal was always clear—just as public school belongs to the public, Nettelhorst belonged to the neighborhood. Parent reformers gambled that the people who lived and worked in the neighborhood would have a vested interest in the school's success and would be willing to work for it. And Nettelhorst's principal had the humility and prudence to ask for help.

Their idea was grand, but hardly grandiose. If neighborhood parents could simply channel their considerable talents toward reforming their neighborhood school, perhaps all the grumbling, finger-pointing, and evasion of responsibility would come to an end. If community members all joined together to help in whatever way they could, perhaps many of the problems that vex public schools would be solved. Of course, fixing what is broken is rarely so simple. Or is it? Change does require investment—investment of time, energy, creativity, guts, perseverance, and even faith. The good news it that in many neighborhoods, these qualities are in limitless supply—they just need to be harnessed.

For well over a century, these positive traits enabled urban neighborhood schools to thrive. Unfortunately, many school boards and policymakers have erroneously concluded that the decline of the urban neighborhood school is inevitable. Ironically, the simplest and cheapest course to school reform has given way to complicated and costly silver bullets: increased centralization, narrow test-based accountability, and resource-draining school choice. Predictably, heavy-handed sticks and underfunded carrots rarely bring about miraculous transformations. The status quo remains. Policymakers offer more regulation and school boards shake sabers, while principals of underperforming and underattended neighborhood schools become ever more insular and adrift. It is no wonder that neighborhood parents look at this tragic situation and take their children (and considerable resources) elsewhere. Whatever side one comes down on in the debates over vouchers, charters, or No Child Left Behind, Nettelhorst proves that the neighborhood school model is still viable.

Given all the fancy new school reform models floating around, the notion of simply asking local communities to reinvest in their neighborhood schools seems positively dowdy. The Nettelhorst movement reveals that a neighborhood school can be quickly and easily rebranded and repositioned to appeal to wary middle-class parents. With a little gussying up, a neighborhood school can be just as desirable as its charter, magnet, or private school counterparts; under solid leadership, it can even evolve to offer a superior product.

One of the most compelling features of the Nettelhorst reform movement is that it succeeded with so little government funding. Nettelhorst's innovative fee-for-service community school, so critical to the success of the project, required only a nominal upfront investment. Beyond the salary for *one* staff member to manage Jane's Place and the funds to cover basic administrative costs, the entire program is completely self-sustaining. The initial financial investment to convert Nettelhorst into a community school was minuscule compared to the social and academic benefits the grant generated. As it is unlikely that America will radically change the way it finances public education anytime soon, neighborhood schools will need all the help they can get to learn how to build strong community relationships and how to identify and leverage resources.

Grassroots reform movements need relatively simple tools to succeed—marketing materials, Internet services, public relations assistance, and accounting services—all of which are affordable and readily available. Just as successful not-for-profit organizations solicit pro bono experts in the private sector, school boards and policymakers could easily encourage local companies to adopt individual schools and provide in-kind goods and services. For example, an accounting firm would likely find it less taxing to chaperone a nearby school's not-for-profit fundraising arm on the side than recruit employees to volunteer as tutors in the school on company time, an advertising agency could easily assign junior associates to develop marketing campaigns for individual schools, and so forth.

Given today's political climate, public schools also need help fundraising. Although Nettelhorst's renaissance did not require much additional public funding, reformers did need the neighborhood's elected leaders to help champion their movement. Fortunately for Nettelhorst, East Lakeview's politicians readily appreciated that *all* of their constituents, regardless of whether they had school-age children at home, had a vested interest in the public school's success.

However, elected officials are not clairvoyant; Nettelhorst needed to learn how to articulate its needs clearly and persuasively, and do the requisite legwork. When it did, neighborhood leaders listened and moved mountains to help the school forge and sustain strong relationships.

Nettelhorst took fundraising to the next level by developing sophisticated, handoff-ready proposals for projects across the educational spectrum. While Nettelhorst parents included many savvy advocates and skilled grant writers, it is unreasonable to expect most schools to be so fortunate. Schools need guidance to help establish "friends of" 501(c)(3) groups. Software that helps facilitate volunteer coordination, community fundraisers, silent auctions, walk-a-thons, and so forth, is readily available, but prohibitive for most individual schools or parent groups. Again, school boards and policymakers could easily develop templates that individual schools could customize and take on the road. Quite simply, it is ludicrous to ask schools to self-finance without giving them the requisite tools to succeed.

Traditionally, school boards have tried to find a great corporate angel who would provide all things to one individual school; a better approach might be to build an association of angels who could offer a group of similar schools expertise and in-kind services aligned with their natural expertise. There is simply no need for reformers to keep reinventing the wheel over and over again.

When the Nettelhorst movement faltered, as it did many, many times, strong relationships—with families, businesses, and community groups  ultimately trumped any negative forces that did not put the needs of children first.

The Nettelhorst renaissance was a big idea for a small school. The Nettelhorst reform movement proves that neighborhood investment can bring about immediate, dramatic, and long-lasting results. Imagine if every neighborhood school could harness the energy that surrounds it to improve education for all children. If all public schools could return to their rightful place as the heart of the community, the Nettelhorst reform movement could indeed become a blueprint for profound and systemic change. Together, a community can create the public school it deserves, and in so doing, change the fabric of the neighborhood for many generations to come.

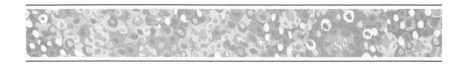

# AFTERWORD

I F WE BUILD IT, they will come. If we teach them, they will learn. We know it can be done, because we have seen it in Chicago.

The Nettelhorst story is not unique; there are hundreds of communities across America struggling to make their schools work. But what makes Nettelhorst a model of successful reform is the group of believers who never took "no" for an answer; the parents who took a leap of faith; the community of small businesses who invested in their neighborhood; and the public school principal and teachers who were determined to fight for change. Together, they changed the lives of hundreds of students and families—and the very direction of their community.

Unfortunately, there are hundreds of communities across the country struggling to keep their elementary schools afloat. That isn't because parents are unwilling or that neighborhoods don't care; it's simply that not every neighborhood is fortunate enough to have the Lakeview community's resources.

The fact is, as schools fail to fulfill their responsibility to their students, taxpayer support diminishes. As motivated parents seek out successful suburban schools, urban schools lose their potential champions. But the reverse can happen, as well. Here in Chicago, we have seen it.

By the mid-1990s, the Chicago public schools were considered to be among the worst in the nation. Academic achievement had flatlined and the system was riddled with waste and inefficiency. But rather than running from the problem, Mayor Richard M. Daley took on the challenge. With leadership from his handpicked school CEOs Paul Vallas and Arne Duncan, the Chicago public schools have dramatically improved. Graduation rates have risen a full 10 percent and reading scores are at an all-time high. There's a lot more work to be done, but we're trending in the right direction. And successful reforms here are providing a model for the nation.

When President Obama laid out his vision for education reform during the campaign, he noted that education is no longer a pathway to opportunity; it has become a *prerequisite* for opportunity. He promised a national investment to improve early childhood education. He called on us to rededicate ourselves to the proposition that every child in this country deserves a world-class education—starting from the day they are born and ending the day they graduate from college. This is critical to their successful futures as individuals. But it's just as critical to our collective future as a nation.

In a 1961 Special Message to Congress on Education, President John F. Kennedy said, "Our progress as a nation can be no swifter than our progress in education. Our requirements for world leadership, our hopes for economic growth, and the demands of citizenship itself in an era such as this all require the maximum development of every young American's capacity. The human mind is our fundamental resource." Fifty years later, under the leadership of a new president, it is time again to answer that call.

As President Obama has said, reforming our education system starts with parents—and the parents at Nettelhorst are a shining example. But all Americans have an obligation to the future of our schools and our students. Education is not only our obligation to the next generation; it is our hope for America's continued world leadership.

If we build it, they will come. If we teach them, they will learn. And when we give them the opportunity, we will succeed as a nation.

—Rahm Emanuel, former member,
United States House of Representatives

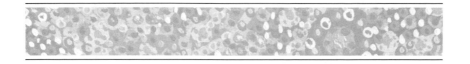

# APPENDIX A

## TOOLKIT: HOW TO SET-UP A 501(C)(3)

Cary Latimer is a Nettelhorst dad of three, and a partner
at Latimer LeVay Jurasek LLC, a Chicago law firm, where
he concentrates his practice in the areas of profit and
not-for-profit corporate planning, complex business
transactions, and estate and wealth planning.

ESTABLISHING an independent fundraising company for your school is a key component of any fundraising effort. There are some legal issues to cover in properly forming the not-for-profit corporation, so you will be required to pay a visit to a locally licensed attorney. The good news is that many local attorneys may be happy to assist you pro bono, meaning the attorney will assist without charging for the attorney's time. A pro bono attorney will generally not cover out-of-pocket expenses, but those expenses are reimbursable from the proceeds of any fundraising efforts. To find an attorney who might be willing to lend a hand, call a local bar association or a local law school's legal aid clinic.

Of course, the usual disclaimer is required here: The information in this section should not be considered legal or tax advice of any kind;

consult an attorney to address specific details and questions. With that disclaimer in mind, here is a brief list of some of the legal issues that will need to be addressed:

**1. Establishing a Not-for-Profit Fundraising Entity.** The key here is establishing a company that is completely independent from the school in a legal respect. Every state has its own laws regarding establishing a not-for-profit corporation. An attorney will be able to assist you in this regard. General information regarding a state's not-for-profit corporations will be available on the website of its secretary of state or Department of Corporations.

Every not-for-profit company will need to have a board of directors (the number of required directors will vary from state to state) and officers (president, treasurer, secretary). No particular experience is needed for the individuals who serve in these capacities; a willingness and commitment to be involved is most important. The not-for-profit corporation will also be required to obtain a federal identification number. An attorney can assist with this matter, but the Internal Revenue Service's website (see www.irs.gov) provides ample guidance to obtain the number.

**2. Obtaining Tax-Exempt Status from the Internal Revenue Service (IRS).** The fundraising entity will be required to obtain tax-exempt status from the Internal Revenue Service, pursuant to Section 501(c)(3) of the Internal Revenue Code. Here again, the assistance of an attorney will be quite helpful. In obtaining the tax-exempt status, a Form 1023 (Application for Recognition of Exemption) will have to be completed and submitted to the Internal Revenue Service. Once the application is submitted, an agent of the IRS will review the application itself and, in all likelihood, contact the attorney or a member of the board of directors to learn more about the fundraising efforts. In order for the tax-exempt status to be granted, the IRS must ultimately be satisfied that the not-for-profit corporation will only have charitable and fundraising objectives. It is not uncommon for the agent of the

IRS to require multiple revisions and modifications to the Form 1023 and ancillary documentation. An example of the Form 1023 is available on the IRS website. Also check for any local regulations or filing requirements that may be applicable to a charitable fundraising not-for-profit corporation. Many states require that the organization make periodic filings to illustrate their fundraising efforts and costs incurred.

This is only an initial guide for how to set up a 501(c)(3), but an attorney will be able to better direct you. Don't be deterred: The process of securing not-for-profit status can be cumbersome, but with a little help from an attorney, most reformers will find that launching a "friends of" organization is not that difficult. Good luck!

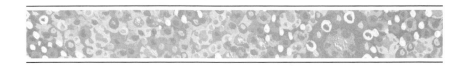

# APPENDIX B

## HOW TO LEARN MORE

To learn more about Community Schools, log on to any of the following websites:

www.communityschools.org
www.afterschoolalliance.org
www.childrensaidsociety.org
www.ascd.org
www.childtrends.org
www.bocyf.org
www.westED.org
www.kettering.org
www.nassembly.org
www.ed.gov
www.acf.hhs.gov
www.mott.org
www.aypf.org
www.cisnet.org
www.forumforyouthinvestment.org
www.ncpie.org
www.ncea.com
www.afterschool.org

To see more pictures of the Nettelhorst School, check out:
www.nettelhorst.org or www.howtowalktoschool.com

To hear Jacqueline and Susan tell their story in their own words, go
to any of the following links:

**Oprah and Friends**: http://www.oprah.com/media/20090115_oaf_
20090115_oaf_nb

**CBS**: http://cbs2chicago.com/video/?id=32179@wbbm.dayport.com

**PBS**: http://nettelhorst.org/news/2006/06/10/nettelhorst-featured-
on-wttw-11/

**NPR**:  http://nettelhorst.org/news/2006/04/26/chicago-matters-
paint-the-walls-hot-pink/

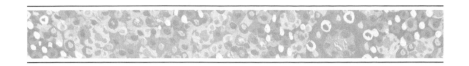

# ABOUT THE AUTHORS

**Jacqueline Edelberg** has been the driving force behind the Nettelhorst School's dramatic turnaround, a story that has been featured on *Oprah & Friends*, NPR, CNN, *60 Minutes*, *Education Weekly*, and in the local Chicago media. A community organizer, writer, and nationally recognized fine artist, Jacqueline has led workshops for the Community Schools Initiative, Northside Parents Network, and Chicago Public Schools on how public schools and reformers can galvanize communities to improve public education. She has consulted with schools and neighborhood groups on issues of strategy and organizational development. Before devoting herself to art, community organizing, and cutting the crusts off bread, Jacqueline taught political science at the University of Osnabrück in Germany as a Fulbright scholar. She earned her bachelor's degree and doctorate from the University of Chicago, and resides in Chicago with her husband, Andrew Slobodien, and their two children, Maya and Zack.

**Susan Kurland** left Nettelhorst to form City Schoolhouse, LLC, a consultancy that advises school communities on best practices. As CEO, she helps principals, parent leaders, and universities develop instructional leadership teams, channel community resources, and formulate health and wellness policies. She has consulted on behalf of the University of

Illinois, the Chicago Public Schools, and the Community Schools' Initiative for the Chicago Community Trust. Susan earned her bachelor's and master's degrees from the City University of New York, and her doctorate from Loyola University of Chicago.

To learn more, please visit www.howtowalktoschool.com or www.nettelhorst.org. To connect with the authors, please email info@howtowalktoschool.com.

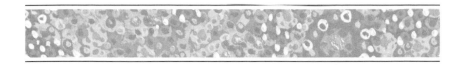

# A CALL TO ACTION

It may feel as though the fate of public education is beyond our control. It is not. Public education belongs to the public—all of us.

As kids, most of us grabbed a lunchbox and a backpack, kissed mom, and headed off to the neighborhood public elementary school. That school, whatever its challenges, helped to shape our character and hopefully instilled in us a lifelong love of learning. Close your eyes for a moment and remember your best friend, see your desk, smell the chalk from freshly clapped erasers, taste a half-chewed pencil, and remember the first teacher who asked you to believe in yourself.

If we all could devote just a small amount of energy to our own neighborhood school, public education in America would transform dramatically—overnight. So gather some friends, walk into your neighborhood school, and ask the principal what you can do to help.

If you are in Chicago, I hope you will come on by. Every Tuesday morning, Laura and I lead tours of Nettelhorst for prospective families; we would love for you to join us. We'll show you where we've been and where we're headed next.

If you are inspired by our work and would like to help keep the momentum going, the Nettelhorst Community Group would be grateful for your support. Know that your contribution will enrich the lives of hundreds of children and will be managed and administered by dedicated parents and professionals. To donate or learn more, log on to www.nettelhorst.org/dreams.

When the original group of eight moms met at the local diner, we hoped that our kids might someday be able to walk to school. We had no idea where this dream would take us. Armed with precariously overloaded strollers, cups of strong coffee, naiveté, moxie, and the roughest of game plans, we kept our heads down and our focus on one goal at a time. I hope our dream inspires you to look to your own sandbox and change the world.

—Jacqueline

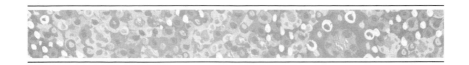

# NOTES

## INTRODUCTION

1. See "An urban education: parents are going to schools to build the city experience they want for their kids," *Chicago Tribune*, June 29, 2008, C3.

2. "An urban education: parents are going to schools to build the city experience they want for their kids," *Chicago Tribune*, June 29, 2008, C3.

## CHAPTER 1

1. After the Nettelhorst reform movement collapsed, Marilyn Eisenberg channeled her considerable energies into cofounding the Chicago Children's Museum; see www.chicagochildrensmuseum.org.

2. A few of Nettelhorst's special education children faced more profound challenges that made inclusion ineffective. While these students spent the majority of their time within their own classrooms, the administration treated them as equal members of the school community.

3. "Harder to get into than Harvard: parents push, plot to get into the best magnet, private and parochial schools in the city," *Chicago Tribune*, February 26, 2008, 1.

4. "Harder to get into than Harvard: parents push, plot to get into the best magnet, private and parochial schools in the city," *Chicago Tribune*, February 26, 2008, 8.

5. "Harder to get into than Harvard: parents push, plot to get into the best magnet, private and parochial schools in the city," *Chicago Tribune*, February 26, 2008, 1.

6. "It's Elementary," *Chicago Magazine*, March 2008, 34.

7. To listen to an interview about the early days of organizing park parents, check out NPR at nettelhorst.org/news/2006/04/26/chicago-matters-paint-the-walls-hot-pink/.

## CHAPTER 2

1. To listen to an interview about the school's renovation, check out NPR at nettelhorst.org/news/2006/04/26/chicago-matters-paint-the-walls-hot-pink/.

2. A few years later, Nettelhorst's front door would become very special, thanks to the work of a gifted Chicago artist, Michael Bonfiglio, aka The Dot Guy; see his work at www.wilddot.com.

3. For some visuals of the school artwork, please see www.nettelhorst.org or check out CBS at cbs2chicago.com/video/?id=32179@wbbm.dayport.com or PBS at nettelhorst.org/news/2006/06/10/nettelhorst-featured-on-wttw-11/.

4. As enrollment increased, parents insisted that the school address its lax security. After Susan retired, Nettelhorst's dynamic new principal, Cindy Wulbert, lobbied the board for an improved security system and insisted that parents sign in and out of the building.

5. See "Why Won't Johnny Eat Broccoli," *Chicago Tribune*, September 26, 2007; see www.purpleasparagus.com/files/trib_sept26_2007.pdf

6. See www.greenmonkeycatering.com.

7. For more on the Hearty Boys, see www.foodnetwork.com/party-line-with-the-hearty-boys/index.html.

8. For more on Nate's makeover see www.nateberkus.com; listen to Nate's interview with Jacqueline, "Making Change in Your Community," on *Oprah & Friends* at www.oprah.com/media/20090115_oaf_20090115_oaf_nb.

## CHAPTER 3

1. For information about the French Market, see www.bensidoun-usa.com.

2. Some key Jane's Place partners did, in fact, pull their satellite classes until the community school could figure out how to schedule classes, collect fees, and supervise programming. Jane's Place filled the void by hiring independent contractors with personal ties to the school community. The school

found that a mix of established institutions and individual artisans actually worked quite well.

## CHAPTER 4

1. When Nettelhorst's tuition-based preschool students (many of whom were children of the early reformers) reached third grade, their test scores ranked among the highest in Chicago, at 100 percent for math and 91 percent for reading.

2. *New York Times*, March 18, 2008, p. A11; see www.teachersunion exposed.com

## CHAPTER 5

1. To learn more about NPN's amazing work, see www.npnparents.org.

2. When Nettelhorst became an International Fine and Performing Arts School and a community school, Kathy helped to reinvent the marketing theme yet again; see www.anexecutivedecision.com.

3. The need for a Jane's Place website was particularly acute because partners were reluctant to promote classes held at Nettelhorst on their own websites until the school could overcome its myriad start-up problems.

4. For example, when the NPN online community discovered a private preschool was packing its chat board with fraudulent reviews, the backlash was fierce; it is doubtful that the school ever fully recovered its reputation.

5. Even when the school upgraded to a new security system, a welcome sign—with instructions—was still necessary.

6. As Nettelhorst's teachers became more accustomed to groups of strangers observing their lessons, Laura Holmes, who had early childhood education training, would join the parent leader on the tour to help highlight some of the academic points as families toured classrooms. Although Laura had become a school employee, her longtime role as Nettelhorst reformer and leader of the Co-op helped to assure parents of her credibility.

7. "At Center of a Clash, Rowdy Children in Coffee Shops, *New York Times*, November 9, 2005; "Hot Type," *Chicago Reader*, November 18, 2005.

8. "Adults-only window display brings a spell of concern," *Chicago Tribune*, March 26, 2006, 1.

9. "Finding a school for kids takes work for gay and lesbian parents in Chicago," *Chicago Free Press*, August 20, 2008; see www.iretiredfromnewsletters .blogspot.com/2008/08/finding-school-for-kids-takes-work-for.html.

## CHAPTER 6

1. See www.alcottschool.net/index.php?option=com_content&task= view&id=347&Itemid=4.

2. The first year, event planners charged $65 per person and $25 for Nettelhorst staff members to attend the silent auction and wine tasting. The following year's admission rose to $75 per person, but remained $25 for teachers. However, that year, if someone wanted to go to the fundraiser, but found the admission price prohibitive, the principal would quietly offer a ticket at cost.

3. FON contributed an extra $2,000 to the first auction proceeds in order to reach the CPS matching goal, and FON president Carol Collier handled all the transfer details with great expediency. The following year, planners convinced FON to invest in professional auction computer software to facilitate the donation process.

4. Reformers didn't know anyone famous themselves, so they asked local public relations firms if they might have anyone they wanted to promote on that day. While reformers were tickled to hijack media coverage, CPS, and especially the mayor's office, did not intend for Principal for a Day to be a three-ring circus. Lesson learned: Mayor Richard M. Daley will not dine with anyone wearing a costume. What is a BZOT? Learn about Dave Skwarczek's amazing creations at www.bzots.com.

5. In fact, Chicago led the nation in philanthropic giving: Households with incomes under $50,000 gave $994; households with incomes from $50,000 to $100,000 gave $911; and households with incomes above $100,000 gave a whopping $1,878. See www.foundationcenter.org.

6. In the 2007–2008 school year, Nettelhorst's student body was 40 percent Caucasian, 25 percent African American, 23 percent Hispanic, 8 percent Asian, 3 percent multiracial, and 1 percent Native American.

7. The Illinois Assembly had approved $500,000 in capital funds to renovate Nettelhorst's auditorium, but at the last minute, the governor redlined the project, a dismaying move considering he announced his tax reform initiative

from a press conference at Nettelhorst. The governor was subsequently impeached and convicted.

8. Like students at many CPS elementary schools, Nettelhorst's students were required to wear a school uniform: navy pants and a white or light blue collared shirt.

9. See www.aplusillinois.org/media/press.asp?pressReleaseID=350.

## CHAPTER 7

1. See "Report Takes Aim at Model Minority Stereotype of Asian American Students," *New York Times*, June 10, 2008, A18.

2. To learn more about Chicago's vibrant East Lakeview neighborhood, see www.lakevieweast.com.

3. The following year, Susan hired Laura and Jane. Laura ran the main office and Jane became the resource coordinator for the community school, Jane's Place at Nettelhorst. Both co-op parents excelled in their new roles and deserve much of the credit for the school's dramatic progress.

4. To learn more about Waters Today and the public school's amazing turn-around, see www.waterstoday.org.